SHAKESPEARE

Edited by A. L. Rowse

Othello

Modern Text with Introduction

UNIVERSITY PRESS OF AMERICA

University Press of America,® Inc.

4720 Boston Way
Lanham, MD 20706

3 Henrietta Street
London WC2E 8LU England

Printed in the United States of America

Distributed to the trade by The Scribner Book Companies

Library of Congress Cataloging in Publication Data

Shakespeare, William, 1564-1616.
Othello

(The Contemporary Shakespeare)
I. Rowse, A. L. (Alfred Leslie), 1903- .
II. Title. III. Series: Shakespeare, William, 1564-1616. Plays (University Press of America : Pbk. ed.)
PR2829.A2R67 1985 822.3'3 85-22764
ISBN 0-8191-3925-4 (pbk.)

This play is also available as part of Volume IV in a seven volume clothbound and slipcased set.

Book design by Leon Bolognese

WHY A CONTEMPORARY SHAKESPEARE?

The starting point of my project was when I learned both from television and in education, that Shakespeare is being increasingly dropped in schools and colleges because of the difficulty of the language. In some cases, I gather, they are given just a synopsis of the play, then the teacher or professor embroiders from his notes.

This is deplorable. We do not want Shakespeare progressively dropped because of superfluous difficulties that can be removed, skilfully, conservatively, keeping to every line of the text. Nor must we look at the question statically, for this state of affairs will worsen as time goes on and we get further away from the language of 400 years ago—difficult enough in all conscience now.

We must begin by ridding our mind of prejudice, i.e. we must not pre-judge the matter. A friend of mine on New York radio said that he was 'appalled' at the very idea; but when he heard my exposition of what was proposed he found it reasonable and convincing.

Just remember, I do not need it myself: *I live in the Elizabethan age*, Shakespeare's time, and have done for years, and am familiar with its language, and his. But even for me there are still difficulties—still more for modern people, whom I am out to help.

Who, precisely?

Not only students at school and in college, but all readers of Shakespeare. Not only those, but all viewers of the plays, in the theatre, on radio and television—actors too, who increasingly find pronunciation of the words difficult, particularly obsolete ones—and there are many, besides the difficulty of accentuation.

The difficulties are naturally far greater for non-English-speaking peoples. We must remember that he is our greatest asset, and that other peoples use him a great deal in learning our language. There are no Iron Curtains for him—though, during Mao's Cultural Revolution in China, he was prohibited. Now that the ban has been lifted, I learn that the Chinese in thousands flock to his plays.

Now, a good deal that was grammatical four hundred years ago is positively ungrammatical today. We might begin by removing what is no longer good grammar.

For example: plural subjects with a verb in the singular:

'*Is* Bushy, Green and the earl of Wiltshire dead?' Any objection to replacing 'is' correctly by 'are'? Certainly not. I notice that some modern editions already correct—

These high wild hills and rough uneven ways
Draw*s* out our miles and make*s* them wearisome

to 'draw' and 'make', quite sensibly. Then, why not go further and regularise this Elizabethan usage to modern, consistently throughout?

Similarly with archaic double negatives—'Nor shall you not think neither'—and double comparatives: 'this is more worser than before.' There are hundreds of instances of what is now just bad grammar to begin with.

There must be a few thousand instances of superfluous subjunctives to reduce to simplicity and sense. Today we use the subjunctive occasionally after 'if', when we say 'if it be'. But we mostly say today 'if it is'. Now Shakespeare has hundreds of subjunctives, not only after if, but after though, although, unless, lest, whether, until, till, etc.

I see no point whatever in retaining them. They only add superfluous trouble in learning English, when the great appeal of our language as a world-language is precisely that it has less grammar to learn than almost any. Russian is unbelievably complicated. Inflected languages—German is like Latin in this respect—are really rather backward; it has been a great recommendation that English has been more progressive in this respect in simplifying itself.

Now we can go further along this line: keep a few subjunctives, if you must, but reduce them to a minimum.

Let us come to the verb. It is a great recommendation to modern English that our verbs are comparatively simple to conjugate—unlike even French, for example. In the Elizabethan age there was a great deal more of it, and some of it inconsistent in modern usage. Take Shakespeare's,

'Where is thy husband now? Where be thy brothers?'

Nothing is lost by rendering this as we should today:

Where is your husband now? Where are your brothers?

And so on.

The second and third person singular—all those shouldsts and wouldsts, wilts and shalts, haths and doths, have become completely obsolete. Here a vast simplification may be effected—with no loss as far as I can see, and with advantages from several points of view.

For example, 'st' at the end of a word is rather difficult to say, and more difficult even for us when it is succeeded by a word beginning with 'th'. Try saying, 'Why usurpedst thou this?' Foreigners have the greatest difficulty in pronouncing our 'th' anyway—many never succeed in getting it round their tongues. Many of these tongue-twisters even for us proliferate in Shakespeare, and I see no objection to getting rid of *superfluous* difficulties. Much easier for people to say, 'Why did you usurp this?'—the same number of syllables too.

This pre-supposes getting rid of almost all thous and thees and thines. I have no objection to keeping a few here and there, if needed for a rhyme—even then they are sometimes not necessary.

Some words in Shakespeare have changed their meaning into the exact opposite: we ought to remove that stumbling-block. When Hamlet says, 'By heaven, I'll make a ghost of him that *lets* me', he means *stops*; and we should replace it by stops, or holds me. Shakespeare regularly uses the word 'owe' where we should say own: the meaning has changed. Take a line like, 'Thou dost here usurp the name thou ow'st not': we should say, 'You do here usurp the name you own not', with the bonus of getting rid of two ugly 'sts'.

The word 'presently' in the Elizabethan age did not mean in a few minutes or so, but immediately—instantly has the same number of syllables. 'Prevent' then had its Latin meaning, to go before, or forestall. Shakespeare frequently uses the word 'still' for always or ever.

Let us take the case of many archaic forms of words, simple one-syllable words that can be replaced without the slightest difference to the scansion: 'sith' for since, 'wrack' for wreck, 'holp' for helped, 'writ' for wrote, 'brake' for broke, 'spake' for spoke, 'bare' for bore, etc.

These give no trouble, nor do a lot of other words that he uses: 'repeal' for recall, 'reproof' for disproof, 'decline' for incline. A few words do give more trouble. The linguistic scholar, C. T. Onions, notes that it is sometimes difficult to give the precise meaning Shakespeare attaches to the word 'conceit'; it usually means thought, or fancy, or concept. I do not know that it ever has our meaning; actually the word 'conceited' with him means ingenious or fantastic, as 'artificial' with Elizabethans meant artistic or ingenious.

There is a whole class of words that have completely gone out, of which moderns do not know the meaning. I find no harm in replacing the word 'coistrel' by rascal, which is what it means—actually it has much the same sound—or 'coil' by fuss; we find 'accite' for summon, 'indigest' for formless. Hamlet's word 'reechy', for the incestuous kisses of his mother and her brother-in-law, has gone out of use: the nearest word, I suppose, would be reeky, but filthy would be a suitable modern equivalent.

In many cases it is extraordinary how little one would need to change, how conservative one could be. Take Hamlet's famous soliloquy, 'To be or not to be.' I find only two words that moderns would not know the meaning of, and one of those we might guess:

> . . .When he himself might his *quietus* make
> With a bare bodkin? Who would *fardels* bear. . .

'Quietus' means put paid; Elizabethans wrote the Latin 'quietus est' at the bottom of a bill that was paid—when it was—to say that it was settled. So that you could replace 'quietus' by settlement, same number of syllables, though not the same accentuation; so I would prefer to use the word acquittance, which has both.

'Fardels' means burdens; I see no objection to rendering, 'Who would burdens bear'—same meaning, same number of syllables, same accent: quite simple. I expect all the ladies to know what a bodkin is: a long pin, or skewer.

Now let us take something really difficult—perhaps the most difficult passage to render in all Shakespeare. It is the virtuoso comic piece describing all the diseases that horseflesh is heir to, in *The Taming of the Shrew*. The horse is Petruchio's. President Reagan tells me that this is the one Shakespearean part that he played—and a very gallant one too. In Britain last year we saw a fine performance of his on horseback in Windsor Park alongside of Queen Elizabeth II—very familiar ground to William Shakespeare and Queen Elizabeth I, as we know from *The Merry Wives of Windsor.*

Here is a headache for us: Petruchio's horse (not President Reagan's steed) was 'possessed with the glanders, and like to mose in the chine; troubled with the lampass, infected with the fashions, full of windgalls, sped with spavins, rayed with the yellows, past cure of the fives, stark spoiled with the staggers, begnawn with the bots; swayed in the back, and shoulder-shotten; near-legged before, and with a half-cheeked bit, and a headstall of sheep's leather', etc.

What on earth are we to make of that? No doubt it raised a laugh with Elizabethans, much more familiarly acquainted with horseflesh than we are; but I doubt if Hollywood was able to produce a nag for Reagan that qualified in all these respects.

Now, even without his horsemanship, we can clear one fence at the outset: 'mose in the chine'. Pages of superfluous commentary have been devoted to that word 'mose'. There was no such Elizabethan word: it was simply a printer's misprint for 'mourn', meaning dripping or running; so it suggests a running sore. You would need to consult the *Oxford English Dictionary*, compiled on historical lines, for some of the words, others like 'glanders' country folk know and we can guess.

So I would suggest a rendering something like this: 'possessed with glanders, and with a running sore in the back; troubled in the gums, and infected in the glands; full of galls in the fetlocks and swollen in the joints; yellow with jaundice, past cure of the strangles; stark spoiled with the staggers, and gnawed by worms; swayed in the back and shoulder put out; near-legged before, and with a half-cheeked bit and headgear of sheep's leather', etc. That at least makes it intelligible.

Oddly enough, one encounters the greatest difficulty with the least important words and phrases, Elizabethan expletives and malapropisms, or salutations like God 'ild you, Godden, for God shield you, Good-even, and so on. 'God's wounds' was Elizabeth I's favourite swearword; it appears frequently enough in Victorian novels as 'Zounds'— I have never heard anyone use it. The word 'Marry!', as in the phrase 'Marry come up!' has similarly gone out, though a very old gentleman at All Souls, Sir Charles Oman, had heard the phrase in the back-streets of Oxford just after the 1914-18 war. 'Whoreson' is frequent on the lips of coarse fellows in Shakespeare: the equivalent in Britain today would be bloody, in America (I suppose) s.o.b.

Relative pronouns, who and which: today we use who for persons, which for things. In Elizabethan times the two were hardly distinguished and were interchangeable. Provokingly Shakespeare used the personal relative 'who' more frequently for impersonal objects, rivers, buildings, towns; and then he no less frequently uses 'which' for persons. This calls out to be regularised for the modern reader.

Other usages are more confusing. The word 'cousin'

was used far more widely by the Elizabethans for their kin: it included nephews, for instance. Thus it is confusing in the English History plays to find a whole lot of nephews—like Richard III's, whom he had made away with in the Tower of London—referred to and addressed as cousins. That needs regularisation today, in the interests of historical accuracy and to get the relationship clear. The word 'niece' was sometimes used of a grandchild—in fact this is the word Shakespeare used in his will for his little grand-daughter Elizabeth, his eventual heiress who ended up as Lady Barnard, leaving money to her poor relations the Hathaways at Stratford. The Latin word *neptis*, from which niece comes also meant grandchild—Shakespeare's grammar-school education at Stratford was in Latin, and this shows you that he often thought of a word in terms of its Latin derivation.

Malapropisms, misuse of words, sometimes mistaking of meanings, are frequent with uneducated people, and sometimes not only with those. Shakespeare transcribed them from lower-class life to raise a laugh, more frequently than any writer for the purpose. They are an endearing feature of the talk of Mistress Quickly, hostess of the Boar's Inn in East Cheapside, and we have no difficulty in making out what she means. But in case some of us do, and for the benefit of non-native English speakers, I propose the correct word in brackets afterwards: 'You have brought her into such a canaries [quandary]. . .and she's as fartuous [virtuous] a civil, modest wife. . .'

Abbreviations: Shakespeare's text is starred—and in my view, marred—by innumerable abbreviations, which not only look ugly on the page but are sometimes difficult to pronounce. It is not easy to pronounce 'is't', or 'in't', or 'on't', and some others: if we cannot get rid of them altogether they should be drastically reduced. Similarly with 'i'th'', 'o'th'', with which the later plays are liberally bespattered, for "in the" or "of the."

We also have a quite unnecessary spattering of apostrophes in practically all editions of the plays—''d' for the past participle, e.g. 'gather'd'. Surely it is much better to regularise the past participle 'ed', e.g. gathered; and when the last syllable is, far less frequently, to be pronounced, then accent it, gatherèd.

This leads into the technical question of scansion, where a practising poet is necessary to get the accents right, to help the reader, and still more the actor. Most people will hardly notice that, very often, the frequent ending of words in 'ion', like reputation, has to be pronounced with two syllables at the end. So I propose to accent this when necessary, e.g. reputatiòn. I have noticed the word 'ocean' as tri-syllabic, so I accent it, to help, oceàn. A number of words which to us are monosyllables were pronounced as two: hour, fire, tired; I sometimes accent or give them a dieresis, either hoùr or fïre. In New England speech words like prayèr, thëre, are apt to be pronounced as two syllables—closer to Elizabethan usage (as with words like gotten) than is modern speech in Britain.

What I notice in practically all editions of Shakespeare's plays is that the editors cannot be relied on to put the accents in the right places. One play edited by a well known Shakespearean editor had, I observed, a dozen accents placed over the wrong syllables. This is understandable, for these people don't write poetry and do not know how to scan. William Shakespeare knew all about scanning, and you need to be both familiar with Elizabethan usage and a practising traditional poet to be able to follow him.

His earlier verse was fairly regular in scansion, mostly iambic pentameter with a great deal of rhyme. As time went on he loosened out, until there are numerous irregular lines—this leaves us much freer in the matter of modernising. Our equivalents should be rhythmically as close as possible, but a strait-jacket need be no part of the equipment. A good Shakespearean scholar tells us, 'there is no necessity for Shakespeare's lines to scan absolutely. He thought of his verse as spoken rather than written and of his rhythmic units in terms of the voice rather than the page.'

There is nothing exclusive or mandatory about my project. We can all read Shakespeare in any edition we like—in the rebarbative olde Englishe spelling of the First Folio, if we wish. Any number of conventional academic editions exist, all weighed down with a burden of notes, many of them superfluous. I propose to make most of them unnecessary—only one occasionally at the foot of very few pages. Let the text be freed of superfluous difficulties, remove obstacles to let it speak for itself, while adhering conservatively to every line.

We really do not need any more editions of the Plays on conventional lines—more than enough of those exist already. But *A Contemporary Shakespeare* on these lines—both revolutionary and conservative—should be a help to everybody all round the world—though especially for younger people, increasingly with time moving away from the language of 400 years ago.

INTRODUCTION

Othello, within its own terms, is a perfect masterpiece; its date 1604, the same year as *Measure for Measure*. Think of turning out two such masterpieces in one year! This play was performed at Court in the old banqueting house at Whitehall on All Saints day, 1 November 1604—other Court performances are recorded. Probably written at home in the country that summer, for we know from John Aubrey that Shakespeare was in the habit of returning to Stratford once a year from the winter's playing in London and (earlier) touring.

Dr. Johnson's judgment was that 'the beauties of this play impress themselves so strongly that they can draw no aid from critical illustration.' What the commonsense of this great writer means is that the play stands in no need of criticism—it speaks for itself. In one sense it is simple, stream-lined, no sub-plot, few characters—unlike the complexities and the large cast of *Hamlet*. Its impact is no less fine, its psychological truth no less searching and revealing, if less complex. Its appeal to other creative artists is far more eloquent than mere criticism, and this has appealed strongly alike to painters and composers. Verdi made a fine opera of it, and indeed the play—like *Macbeth*—moves like an opera.

Shakespeare's contemporary, even the critical Ben Jonson, allowed that 'he was not for an age, but for all time'—a true prophecy. And *Othello* points to a prime issue of our own day, that of race relations. Just as *The Merchant of Venice* highlights the Jewish question and anti-Semitism, so *Othello* underscores the relation between black and white. Actually Othello is not a negro, though he calls himself 'black'; he is a Moor, of North Africa.

Nevertheless, the tragedy between Othello and Desdemona is due to this. Deeply in love with this very masculine, soldierly man, years older than herself, she did wrong in marrying him; for this was against her father's will, and that was a serious offence to sixteenth century minds. It exposed her to the disapprobation of her friends, and left her alone, face to face with a very passionate and unreasonable man, himself exposed to the envy of others, and within himself to his own sense of inferiority on account of race and age: an easy victim because of the simplicity, devotion and magnanimity of his own nature. He murders out of excessive love, turned to jealousy by the machinations of an envious, evil man.

Iago is by far the most interesting character in the play, a fascinating psychological study for those interested in such things. He is often presented as a man of motiveless malignity, a monster of mere evil. This is inadequate: he has his motives—he has been downgraded by Othello—and his suspicions, for he suspects Othello with his wife. But *he* is not motivated by sexual jealousy; like Richard III, he is rather strait-laced—a type that did not commend itself to the very sexy Shakespeare. He belongs to that rare kind of person who hates the sight of other people's happiness—that is to say, he is not incredible, a monster: he is real, but rare.

He also hates human beings for their foolery—and this too is understandable, if rare: Swift understood it all right. One cannot but admire the sheer skill with which he takes in fool after fool—beginning with the silly gentleman Roderigo, who aspires to Desdemona's favours. Well, if people like to be such fools, they get what is coming to them —and they should certainly keep out of the way of a clever, scheming villain like Iago. 'Thus credulous fools are caught', he sums up: he had no compunction or mercy for their credulity—serve them out for it would be his attitude.

All the same, it *is* terrible to watch Othello falling into his snare. Terrible, and also fascinating, for Iago sails so brazenly, so truthfully, close to the wind. Like Hitler, Iago knows that to tell human fools the truth is often the most effective way of taking them in. He actually warns Othello of the danger of being jealous—Othello of course thinks him all the more honest for that. He speaks a good word to Othello on behalf of Cassio whom he means to destroy: Othello believes him all the more when it comes to sowing suspicion as to Cassio's relations with Othello's wife. 'Honest Iago' is his misnomer. And of course the simple, innocent girl that Desdemona is becomes a helpless victim in such hands. One is torn with compassion as one watches the bird fluttering into the net; one's heart turns over at the final act of the tragedy in her bed-chamber, her last talk with the faithful Emilia (that name!)—who has also been an innocent instrument in bringing it about—her total incomprehension of why such a fate has come upon her.

Shakespeare got the well-known story from an Italian *novella,* one of Cinthio's again; but, as Sisson reminds us, he transformed what was 'a brutal and vulgar story' in the original by 'the splendour of his art.' It reminds one of the transformation he wrought from Arthur Brooke's pedestrian poem into *Romeo and Juliet,* with which *Othello* may profitably be compared.

More of the age is reflected in the later play. Desdemona's father can account for her falling for the Moor only by witchcraft or charms, spells or drugs. Jacobean society was very conscious of this kind of thing, with the King himself such an authority on witches, and such people as 'Dr.' Forman so successful in London (Ben Jonson put him into *The*

Alchemist). In a few years Forman would be compounding love-philtres for the wicked young Countess of Essex to compel the love of the King's boy-friend, Robert Carr, fatally towards herself. The handkerchief given to Othello's mother by an Egyptian charmer—which Desdemona lost so suspiciously—had a magical potency:

> The worms were hallowed that did breed the silk,
> And it was dyed in mummy—

supposed to have been concocted from mummies (what credulity!), and Forman dealt also in that. He had had a good record for sticking to his post in plague-time, when orthodox doctors absconded from London. The year 1603 saw one of the severe decennial visitations, and we see it in the background in the image:

> As does the raven over the infected house
> Boding to all.

Other images bring the time clearly before us. Othello's marriage, for instance:

> Faith, tonight he has boarded a land carrack:
> If it proves lawful prize, he's made for ever.

We note the doubt upon the marriage from the first; but carracks were the contemporary Portuguese ships bringing the treasures of the East to Europe. The Elizabethans boarded and made prizes of several, notably the *Madre de Dios*, taken by Ralegh's ships.

> The Anthropophagi, and men whose heads
> Do grow beneath their shoulders—

this observation lodged in the mind of that reading man,[1] the dramatist, from Ralegh's *Discovery . . . of Guiana* of 1596. The description of the Hellespont and the Pontic Sea came straight from Philemon Holland's translation of Pliny.

From the beginning Shakespeare had always had a leaning to grand language—in itself an index to his character: the style is the man. With the plays of this late-middle period we see the addiction to rare words and idiosyncratic phrases growing upon him, until we come to the difficult, elliptical, eccentric language of the last plays. *Othello* already provides many examples of rare words—all the more necessary to give them modern equivalents, for few know what they mean. No one else seems ever to have used the word 'exsufflicate' for inflated, or 'antres' for caves. We are used to the grand words he liked to use, like 'conjunctive', 'sequent messengers', 'iterance' for repetition, 'indign' for unworthy, 'portance' for conduct. But why accept unnecessary difficulty with such forms as 'ingredience' for ingredients, 'arrivance' for arrivals, 're-stem' for retrace, 'injointed' for united, 'designment' for design, etc.? Who but Shakespeare would use the word 'fortitude' for the strength of a place; or 'my speculative and officed instruments', to mean my visual and (other) usual faculties? Or we may take a more simple example to illustrate the necessity of removing obscurities where possible: 'Be not acknown on't' is here rendered simply, 'Acknowledge it not.'

---

[1]cf. my *What Shakespeare Read and Thought.*

CHARACTERS

OTHELLO, a Moor in the service of Venice
DESDEMONA, his wife
CASSIO, his Lieutenant
IAGO, his Ancient, i.e. Ensign
EMILIA, wife of Iago
BIANCA, mistress of Cassio
RODERIGO, a Venetian gentleman
THE DUKE OF VENICE
BRABANTIO, a Venetian Senator, Desdemona's father
GRATIANO, his brother
LODOVICO, his kinsman
MONTANO, Governor of Cyprus

Senators, Gentlemen, Musicians, Officers, Attendants.

Act I

SCENE I
Venice. Before Brabantio's house.

Enter Roderigo and Iago

RODERIGO
Tush, never tell me! I take it much unkindly
That you, Iago, who have had my purse
As if the strings were yours, should know of this.

IAGO
God, but you will not hear me!
If ever I did dream of such a matter,
Abhor me.

RODERIGO
You told me you did hold him in your hate.

IAGO
Despise me, if I do not. Three great ones of the city,
In personal suit to make me his Lieutenant,
Off-capped to him: and by the faith of man,
I know my price, I am worth no worse a place.
But he, as loving his own pride and purposes,
Evades them with a bombast circumstance
Horribly stuffed with epithets of war,
And in conclusion
Non-suits my mediators. For 'Sure,' says he,
'I have already chosen my officer.'
And what was he?
Indeed, a great arithmeticiàn,
One Michael Cassio, a Florentine—
A fellow almost damned in a fair wife—

That never set a squadron in the field,
Nor the division of an army knows
More than a spinster—unless the bookish theory,
Wherein the togaed consuls can propose
As masterly as he. Mere prattle without practice
Is all his soldiership. But he, sir, had the election.
And I, of whom his eyes had seen the proof
At Rhodes, at Cyprus, and on other grounds
Christian and heathen, must be leed and calmed
By debitor and creditor. This counter-caster,
He in good time must his Lieutenant be,
And I—God bless the mark!—his Moorship's Ensign.

RODERIGO

By heaven, I rather would have been his hangman.

IAGO

Why, there's no remedy. It is the curse of service:
Preferment goes by letter and affection,
And not by old gradation, where each second
Stood heir to the first. Now sir, be judge yourself
Whether I in any just term am obliged
To love the Moor.

RODERIGO

I would not follow him then.

IAGO O, sir, content you:

I follow him to serve my turn upon him.
We cannot all be masters, nor all masters
Cannot be truly followed. You shall mark
Many a duteous and knee-crooking knave
That, doting on his own obsequious bondage,
Wears out his time, much like his master's ass,
For naught but provender, and when he's old—cashiered!
Whip me such honest knaves. Others there are
Who, trimmed in forms and visages of duty,
Keep yet their hearts attending on themselves,
And, throwing but shows of service on their lords,

Do thrive by them; and when they have lined their coats,
Do themselves homage. These fellows have some soul,
And such a one do I profess myself.
For, sir,
It is as sure as you are Roderigo,
Were I the Moor, I would not be Iago:
In following him, I follow but myself.
Heaven is my judge, not I for love and duty,
But seeming so for my peculiar end:
For when my outward action demonstrates
The native act and figure of my heart
In compliment extern, 'tis not long after,
But I will wear my heart upon my sleeve
For daws to peck at. I am not what I am.

RODERIGO
What a full fortune does the thick-lips own
If he can carry it thus!

IAGO Call up her father,
Rouse him, make after him, poison his delight,
Proclaim him in the streets; incense her kinsmen,
And, though he in a fertile climate dwells,
Plague him with flies; though now his joy is joy,
Yet throw such chances of vexation on it,
As it may lose some colour.

RODERIGO
Here is her father's house; I'll call aloud.

IAGO
Do, with like fearsome accent and dire yell,
As when, by night and negligence, the fire
Is spied in populous cities.

RODERIGO
What, ho, Brabantio! Signior Brabantio, ho!

IAGO

Awake! What, ho, Brabantio! Thieves, thieves!
Look to your house, your daughter, and your bags!
Thieves, thieves!

Enter Brabantio above at a window

BRABANTIO

What is the reason of this terrible summons?
What is the matter there?

RODERIGO

Signior, is all your family within?

IAGO

Are your doors locked?

BRABANTIO Why, wherefore ask you this?

IAGO

Zounds, sir, you're robbed; for shame, put on your gown;
Your heart is burst, you have lost half your soul.
Even now, now, very now, an old black ram
Is tupping your white ewe. Arise, arise,
Awake the snorting citizens with the bell,
Or else the devil will make a grandsire of you.
Arise, I say!

BRABANTIO What, have you lost your wits?

RODERIGO

Most reverend signior, do you know my voice?

BRABANTIO

Not I: what are you?

RODERIGO My name is Roderigo.

BRABANTIO

The worser welcome!
I have charged you not to haunt about my doors.
In honest plainness you have heard me say
My daughter is not for you. And now in madness,
Being full of supper and distempering draughts,

Upon malicious bravery do you come
To startle my quiet.

RODERIGO
Sir, sir, sir—

BRABANTIO But you must needs be sure
My spirit and my place have in them power
To make this bitter to you.

RODERIGO Patience, good sir.

BRABANTIO
What tell you me of robbing? This is Venice:
My house is not a grange.

RODERIGO Most grave Brabantio,
In simple and pure soul I come to you . . .

IAGO Zounds, sir, you are one of those that will not serve God if the devil bids you. Because we come to do you service, and you think we are ruffians, you'll have your daughter covered with a Barbary horse; you'll have your nephews neigh to you, you'll have coursers for cousins, and jennets for kin.

BRABANTIO What profane wretch are you?

IAGO I am one, sir, that comes to tell you, your daughter and the Moor are now making the beast with two backs.

BRABANTIO
You are a villain.

IAGO You are a Senator.

BRABANTIO
This you shall answer. I know you, Roderigo.

RODERIGO
Sir, I will answer anything. But I beseech you
If it is your pleasure and most wise consent,
As partly I find it is, that your fair daughter,
At this odd-even and dull watch of the night,
Transported with no worse nor better guard
But with a knave of common hire, a gondolier,
To the gross clasps of a lascivious Moor—

If this is known to you, and your allowance,
We then have done you bold and saucy wrongs.
But if you know not this, my manners tell me
We have your wrong rebuke. Do not believe
That from the sense of all civility
I thus would play and trifle with your reverence.
Your daughter, if you have not given her leave,
I say again has made a gross revolt,
Tying her duty, beauty, wit, and fortunes
In an extravagant and wheeling stranger
Of here and everywhere. Straight satisfy yourself:
If she is in her chamber or your house,
Let loose on me the justice of the state
For thus deluding you.

BRABANTIO Strike on the tinder, ho!
Give me a taper; call up all my people!
This accident is not unlike my dream:
Belief of it oppresses me already.
Light, I say, light! *Exit above*

IAGO Farewell, for I must leave you.
It seems not meet, nor wholesome to my place,
To be produced—as if I stay, I shall—
Against the Moor. For I do know the state,
However this may gall him with some check,
Cannot with safety sack him. For he's embarked
With such loud reason to the Cyprus wars,
Which even now stand in act, that for their souls
Another of his fathom they have none
To lead their business. In which regard,
Though I do hate him as I do hell pains,
Yet for necessity of present life
I must show out a flag and sign of love,
Which is indeed but sign. That you shall surely find him,
Lead to the Sagittary the raisèd search;
And there will I be with him. So farewell. *Exit*

Enter Brabantio below with servants and torches

BRABANTIO

It is too true an evil. Gone she is,
And what's to come of my despisèd time
Is naught but bitterness. Now, Roderigo,
Where did you see her?—O unhappy girl!—
With the Moor, say you?—Who would be a father?—
How did you know it was she?—She deceives me
Past thought!—What said she to you?—Get more tapers.
Raise all my kindred.—Are they married, think you?

RODERIGO

Truly I think they are.

BRABANTIO

O heaven! How got she out? O treason of the blood!
Fathers, from hence trust not your daughters' minds
By what you see them act. Are there not charms
By which the property of youth and maidenhood
May be abused? Have you not read, Roderigo,
Of some such thing?

RODERIGO Yes, sir, I have indeed.

BRABANTIO

Call up my brother—O would you had had her!
Some one way, some another. Do you know
Where we may apprehend her and the Moor?

RODERIGO

I think I can discover him, if you please
To get good guard and go along with me.

BRABANTIO

Pray you, lead on. At every house I'll call—
I may command at most. Get weapons, ho!
And raise some special officers of night.
On, good Roderigo, I'll reward your pains. *Exeunt*

SCENE II
A street.

Enter Othello, Iago, attendants with torches

IAGO
Though in the trade of war I have slain men,
Yet do I hold it very stuff of the conscience
To do no contrived murder: I lack iniquity
Sometimes to do me service. Nine or ten times
I had thought to yerk him here under the ribs.

OTHELLO
It is better as it is.

IAGO Nay, but he prated
And spoke such scurvy and provoking terms
Against your honour,
That with the little godliness I have,
I did full hard forbear him. But I pray, sir,
Are you fast married? For be assured of this,
That the Magnifico is much beloved,
And has in his effect a voice potential
As double as the Duke's. He will divorce you,
Or put upon you what restraint and grievance
That law, with all its might to enforce it on,
Will give him cable.

OTHELLO Let him do his spite:
My services, which I have done the signiory,
Shall out-tongue his complaints. It is not yet known—
That, when I know that boasting is an honour,
I shall promùlgate—I fetch my life and being
From men of royal rank, and my demerits
May speak, unbonneted, to as proud a fortune
As this that I have reached. For know, Iago,
But that I love the gentle Desdemona,
I would not my unhousèd free condition

Put into circumscription and confine
For the seas' worth. But look, what lights come there!

IAGO
Those are the raisèd father and his friends:
You were best go in.

OTHELLO Not I: I must be found.
My parts, my title, and my perfect soul
Shall manifest me rightly. Is it they?

IAGO
By Janus, I think no.

Enter Cassio, with men bearing torches

OTHELLO
The servants of the Duke and my Lieutenant!
The goodness of the night upon you, friends.
What is the news?

CASSIO The Duke does greet you, General,
And he requires your haste-post-haste appearance
Even on the instant.

OTHELLO What is the matter, think you?

CASSIO
Something from Cyprus, as I may divine:
It is a business of some heat. The galleys
Have sent a dozen sequent messengers
This very night at one another's heels;
And many of the consuls, raised and met,
Are at the Duke's already. You have been hotly called for,
When being not at your lodging to be found.
The senate has sent about three several quests
To search you out.

OTHELLO 'Tis well I am found by you:
I will but spend a word here in the house
And go with you. *Exit*

CASSIO Ensign, what makes he here?

IAGO

Faith, he tonight has boarded a land carack:
If it proves lawful prize, he's made for ever.

CASSIO

I do not understand.

IAGO He's married.

CASSIO To whom?

IAGO

Marry, to—Come, Captain, will you go?

Enter Othello

OTHELLO Along with you.

CASSIO

Here comes another troop to seek for you.

Enter Brabantio, Roderigo, with officers and torches

IAGO

It is Brabantio: General, be advised,
He comes to bad intent.

OTHELLO Holla, stand there.

RODERIGO

Signior, it is the Moor.

BRABANTIO Down with him, thief!

IAGO

You, Roderigo? Come, sir, I am for you.

OTHELLO

Keep up your bright swords, for the dew will rust them.
Good signior, you shall more command with years
Than with your weapons.

BRABANTIO

O you foul thief! Where have you stowed my daughter?
Damned as you are, you have enchanted her.
For I'll refer me to all things of sense,

If she in chains of magic is not bound,
Whether a maid, so tender, fair, and happy,
So opposite to marriage that she shunned
The wealthy curlèd darlings of our nation,
Would ever have—to incur a general mock—
Run from her wardship to the sooty bosom
Of such a thing as you. To fear, not to delight.
Judge me the world, if 'tis not gross in sense
That you have practised on her with foul charms,
Abused her delicate youth with drugs or minerals
That weaken willpower. I'll have it disputed on;
'Tis probable, and palpable to thinking.
I therefore apprehend, and do attach you
For an abuser of the world, a practiser
Of arts inhibited, and out of warrant.
Lay hold upon him: if he does resist,
Subdue him, at his peril.

OTHELLO Hold your hands,
Both you of my inclining and the rest.
Were it my cue to fight, I should have known it
Without a prompter. Where will you that I go
To answer this your charge?

BRABANTIO To prison, till fit time
Of law and course of direct sessiòn
Calls you to answer.

OTHELLO What if I do obey?
How may the Duke be therewith satisfied,
Whose messengers are here about my side,
Upon some urgent business of the state
To bring me to him?

OFFICER 'Tis true, most worthy signior:
The Duke's in council, and your noble self
I am sure is sent for.

BRABANTIO How? The Duke in council?
In this time of the night? Bring him away.
Mine's not an idle cause; the Duke himself,

Or any of my brothers of the state,
Cannot but feel this wrong as if their own:
For if such actions may have passage free,
Bondslaves and pagans shall our statesmen be. *Exeunt*

SCENE III
The Duke's palace.

The Duke and Senators at table with lights and attendants

DUKE
There is no consistency in these news
That gives them credit.
FIRST SENATOR Indeed they are inconsistent.
My letters say a hundred and seven galleys.
DUKE
And mine, a hundred and forty.
SECOND SENATOR And mine two hundred;
But though they tally not on a just account—
As in these cases where the aim reports
'Tis oft with difference—yet do they all confirm
A Turkish fleet, and bearing up to Cyprus.
DUKE
Nay, it is possible enough to judgement:
I do not so secure me in the error,
But the main article I do approve
In fearful sense.
SAILOR (*without*) What, ho! What, ho! What, ho!
FIRST OFFICER
A messenger from the galleys.

Enter Sailor

DUKE Now, what's the business?

SAILOR

The Turkish preparation makes for Rhodes;
So was I bid report here to the state
By Signior Angelo.

DUKE

How say you by this change?

FIRST SENATOR This cannot be,
By any test of reason. It is a pageant
To keep us in false gaze. When we consider
The importance of Cyprus to the Turk,
And let ourselves again but understand
That as it more concerns the Turk than Rhodes,
So may he with more facile question bear it:
Because it stands not in such warlike brace,
But altogether lacks the abilities
That Rhodes is dressed in. If we make thought of this,
We must not think the Turk is so unskilful
To leave that latest which concerns him first,
Neglecting an attempt of ease and gain
To wake and wage a danger profitless.

DUKE

Nay, in all confidence he's not for Rhodes.

FIRST OFFICER

Here is more news.

Enter a Messenger

MESSENGER

The Ottomites, reverend and gracious,
Steering with due course toward the isle of Rhodes,
Have there united with an after-fleet.

FIRST SENATOR

Ay, so I thought. How many, as you guess?

MESSENGER
Of thirty sail; and now they do retrace
Their backward course, bearing with frank appearance
Their purposes toward Cyprus. Signior Montano,
Your trusty and most valiant servitor,
With his free duty recommends you thus,
And prays you to believe him.

DUKE
It is certain then for Cyprus.
Marcus Luccicos, is not he in town?

FIRST SENATOR
He is now in Florence.

DUKE Write from us: wish him
Post-post-haste dispatch.

FIRST SENATOR
Here comes Brabantio and the valiant Moor.

Enter Brabantio, Othello, Iago, Roderigo, and officers

DUKE
Valiant Othello, we must straight employ you
Against the general enemy Ottoman.
(*To Brabantio*) I did not see you: welcome, gentle signior;
We lacked your counsel and your help tonight.

BRABANTIO
So did I yours. Good your grace, pardon me:
Neither my place, nor aught I heard of business,
Has raised me from my bed; nor does the general care
Take hold on me. For my particular grief
Is of so flood-gate and overbearing nature
That it engulfs and swallows other sorrows
And yet is still itself.

DUKE Why? What's the matter?

BRABANTIO
My daughter! O, my daughter!

SENATORS Dead?

BRABANTIO Ay, to me.
She is abused, stolen from me, and corrupted
By spells and medicines bought of mountebanks;
For nature so preposterously to err,
Being not deficient, blind, or lame of sense,
Without witchcraft could not.

DUKE
Whoever he is that in this foul proceeding
Has thus beguiled your daughter of herself
And you of her, the bloody book of law
You shall yourself read in the bitter letter
After your own sense—yea, though our very son
Stood in your action.

BRABANTIO Humbly I thank your grace.
Here is the man: this Moor, whom now it seems
Your special mandate for the state affairs
Has hither brought.

ALL We are very sorry for it.

DUKE
What in your own part can you say to this?

BRABANTIO
Nothing, but this is so.

OTHELLO
Most potent, grave and reverend signiors,
My very noble and approved good masters,
That I have taken away this old man's daughter,
It is most true. True I have married her;
The very head and front of my offending
Has this extent, no more. Rude am I in my speech
And little blessed with the soft phrase of peace;
For since these arms of mine had seven years' pith
Till now some nine moons wasted, they have used
Their dearest action in the tented field.
And little of this great world can I speak
More than pertains to feats of broil and battle;
And therefore little shall I grace my cause

In speaking for myself. Yet, by your gracious patience.
I will a round unvarnished tale deliver
Of my whole course of love: what drugs, what charms,
What conjuration and what mighty magic—
For such proceedings I am charged with too—
I won his daughter.

BRABANTIO A maiden never bold;
Of spirit so still and quiet that her motion
Blushed at herself: and she, in spite of nature,
Of years, of country, credit, everything,
To fall in love with what she feared to look on!
It is a judgement maimed and most imperfect
That will confess perfection so could err
Against all rules of nature, and must be driven
To find out practices of cunning hell
Why this should be. I therefore vowed again
That with some mixtures powerful o'er the blood,
Or with some dram conjured to this effect,
He wrought upon her.

DUKE To vouch this is no proof,
Without much wider and more overt test
Than these thin habits and poor likelihoods
Of common seeming do prefer against him.

FIRST SENATOR
But, Othello, speak:
Did you by indirect and forcèd courses
Subdue and poison this young maid's affections?
Or came it by request and such fair question
As soul to soul affords?

OTHELLO I do beseech you,
Send for the lady to the Sagittary,
And let her speak of me before her father.
If you do find me foul in her report,
The trust, the office I do hold of you
Not only take away, but let your sentence
Even fall upon my life.

DUKE Fetch Desdemona hither.

OTHELLO

Ensign, conduct them: you best know the place.

Exit Iago with attendants

And till she comes, as truly as to heaven
I do confess the vices of my blood,
So justly to your grave ears I'll present
How I did thrive in this fair lady's love,
And she in mine.

DUKE Say it, Othello.

OTHELLO

Her father loved me, oft invited me,
Ever questioned me the story of my life
From year to year—the battles, sieges, fortunes
That I have passed.
I ran it through, even from my boyish days
To the very moment that he bade me tell it.
Wherein I spoke of most disastrous chances,
Of moving accidents by flood and field,
Of hair-breadth escapes in the imminent deadly breach,
Of being taken by the insolent foe,
And sold to slavery; of my redemption thence,
And conduct in my travels' history.
Wherein of caverns vast and deserts idle,
Rough quarries, rocks, and hills whose heads touch heaven,
It was my hint to speak—such was the process.
And of the cannibals that each other eat,
The anthropophagi, and men whose heads
Do grow beneath their shoulders. This to hear
Would Desdemona seriously incline.
But still the house affairs would draw her thence,
Which ever as she could with haste dispatch
She'd come again, and with a greedy ear
Devour up my discourse. This I observing
Took once a pliant hour, and found good means

To draw from her a prayer of earnest heart
That I would all my pilgrimage dilate,
Whereof by parcels she had something heard,
But not attentively. I did consent,
And often did beguile her of her tears
When I did speak of some distressful stroke
That my youth suffered. My story being done,
She gave me for my pains a world of sighs:
She swore, in faith 'twas strange, 'twas passing strange,
'Twas pitiful, 'twas wondrous pitiful;
She wished she had not heard it, yet she wished
That heaven had made her such a man. She thanked me,
And bade me, if I had a friend that loved her,
I should but teach him how to tell my story,
And that would woo her. Upon this hint I spoke:
She loved me for the dangers I had passed,
And I loved her, that she did pity them.
This only is the witchcraft I have used.
Here comes the lady: let her witness it.

Enter Desdemona, Iago, and attendants

DUKE
I think this tale would win my daughter too.
Good Brabantio, take up this mangled matter at the best:
Men do their broken weapons rather use
Than their bare hands.

BRABANTIO I pray you hear her speak.
If she confesses that she was half the wooer,
Destruction on my head, if my bad blame
Light on the man! Come hither, gentle mistress;
Do you perceive in all this company
Where most you owe obedience?

DESDEMONA My noble father,
I do perceive here a divided duty:
To you I am bound for life and education;
My life and education both do teach me
How to respect you. You are lord of all my duty,
I am hitherto your daughter. But here's my husband;
And so much duty as my mother showed
To you, preferring you before her father,
So much I challenge, that I may profess
Due to the Moor, my lord.

BRABANTIO Goodbye! I have done.
Please it your grace, on to the state affairs.
I had rather to adopt a child than get it.
Come hither, Moor:
I here do give you that with all my heart
What, but you have already, with all my heart
I would keep from you. For your sake, jewel,
I am glad at soul I have no other child,
For your escape would teach me tyranny
To hang clogs on them. I have done, my lord.

DUKE
Let me speak like yourself and lay a sentence
Which as a ladder or step may help these lovers
Into your favour.
When remedies are past the griefs are ended
By seeing the worst which late on hopes depended.
To mourn a mischief that is past and gone
Is the next way to draw new mischief on.
What cannot be preserved when fortune takes,
Patience her injury a mockery makes.
The robbed that smiles steals something from the thief;
He robs himself that spends a useless grief.

BRABANTIO
So let the Turk of Cyprus us beguile,
We lose it not so long as we can smile;
He bears the sentence well that nothing bears

But the free comfort which from thence he hears;
But he bears both the sentence and the sorrow
That to pay grief must of poor patience borrow.
These sentences, to sugar or to gall
Being strong on both sides, are equivocal.
But words are words; I never yet did hear
That the bruised heart was mended through the ear.
I humbly beseech you proceed to the affairs of state.

DUKE The Turk with a most mighty preparation makes for Cyprus. Othello, the strength of the place is best known to you: and though we have there a substitute of most allowed sufficiency, yet opinion, a more sovereign mistress of effects, throws a safer voice on you. You must therefore be content to darken the gloss of your new fortunes with this more stubborn and boisterous expedition.

OTHELLO
The tyrant, custom, most grave Senators,
Has made the flinty and steel couch of war
My thrice-driven bed of down. I do acknowledge
A natural and prompt alacrity
I find in hardness; and do undertake
This present war against the Ottomites.
Most humbly, therefore, bending to your state,
I crave fit disposition for my wife,
Due reference of place, provision too.
With such accommodation and attendance
As levels with her breeding.

DUKE If you please,
Be it at her father's.

BRABANTIO I will not have it so.

OTHELLO
Nor I.

DESDEMONA Nor I: I would not there reside
To put my father in impatient thoughts
By being in his eye. Most gracious Duke,

To my unfolding lend your prosperous ear,
And let me find a charter in your voice
To assist my simpleness.

DUKE What would you? Speak.

DESDEMONA

That I did love the Moor to live with him,
My downright violence and storm of fortunes
May trumpet to the world. My heart is subdued
Even to the very quality of my lord.
I saw Othello's visage in his mind,
And to his honours and his valiant parts
Did I my soul and fortunes consecrate.
So that, dear lords, if I am left behind
A moth of peace, and he goes to the war,
The rites for which I love him are bereft me;
And I a heavy interim shall support
By his dear absence. Let me go with him.

OTHELLO

Let her have your voice.
Hear with me, heaven, I therefore beg it not
To please the palate of my appetite,
Nor to comply with heat—the young desires
In me defunct—and my own satisfaction;
But to be free and bounteous to her mind.
And heaven defend your good souls that you think
I will your serious and great business scant
Because she is with me. No, when light-winged toys
Of feathered Cupid blind with wanton dullness
My visual and other faculties,
That pleasure may corrupt and taint my business—
Let housewives make a skillet of my helm,
And all unworthy and base adversities
Make head against my reputatiòn!

DUKE
Be it as you shall privately determine,
Either for her stay, or going. The affair cries haste,
And speed must answer it. You must hence tonight.

DESDEMONA
Tonight, my lord?

DUKE This night.

OTHELLO With all my heart.

DUKE
At nine in the morning, here we'll meet again.
Othello, leave some officer behind,
And he shall our commission bring to you,
With such things else of quality and respect
As do concern you.

OTHELLO So please your grace, my Ensign.
A man he is of honesty and trust:
To his conveyance I assign my wife,
With what else needful your good grace shall think
To be sent after me.

DUKE Let it be so.
Good night to everyone. And, noble signior,
If virtue no delighted beauty lack,
Your son-in-law is far more fair than black.

FIRST SENATOR
Adieu, brave Moor: use Desdemona well.

BRABANTIO
Look to her, Moor, if you have eyes to see.
She has deceived her father, and may thee.

OTHELLO
My life upon her faith!

Exeunt Duke, Senators, and attendants

Honest Iago,
My Desdemona must I leave to you.
I pray you let your wife attend on her,
And bring them after in the best advantage.
Come, Desdemona, I have but an hour

Of love, of worldly matters and direction
To spend with you. We must obey the time.
Exeunt Othello and Desdemona

RODERIGO Iago.

IAGO What say you, noble heart?

RODERIGO What will I do, think you?

IAGO Why, go to bed and sleep.

RODERIGO I will incontinently drown myself.

IAGO If you do, I shall never love you after. Why, you silly gentleman!

RODERIGO It is silliness to live, when to live is torment: and then we have a prescription to die, when death is our physician.

IAGO O villainous! I have looked upon the world for four times seven years, and since I could distinguish between a benefit and an injury, I never found a man that knew how to love himself. Ere I would say I would drown myself for the love of a guinea-hen, I would change my humanity with a baboon.

RODERIGO What should I do? I confess it is my shame to be so foolish, but it is not in my virtue to amend it.

IAGO Virtue? A fig! 'Tis in ourselves that we are thus, or thus. Our bodies are our gardens, to which our wills are gardeners. So that if we will plant nettles or sow lettuce, set hyssop and weed up thyme, supply it with one gender of herbs or distract it with many, either to have it sterile with idleness or manured with industry, why the power and corrigible authority of this lies in our wills. If the beam of our lives had not one scale of reason to poise another of sensuality, the blood and baseness of our natures would conduct us to most preposterous conclusions. But we have reason to cool our raging motions, our carnal stings, our unbitted lusts: whereof I take this, that you call love, to be a sect or scion.

RODERIGO It cannot be.

IAGO It is merely a lust of the blood and a permission of the will. Come, be a man. Drown yourself? Drown cats and blind puppies. I have professed me your friend, and I confess me knit to your deserving with cables of perdurable toughness. I could never better help you than now. Put money in your purse. Follow you these wars; disguise your face with an usurped beard. I say, put money in your purse. It cannot be that Desdemona should long continue her love to the Moor—put money in your purse—nor he his to her. It was a violent commencement, and you shall see an answerable sequestration—put but money in your purse. These Moors are changeable in their wills—fill your purse with money. The food that to him now is as luscious as locusts shall be to him shortly as bitter as quinine. She must change for youth: when she is sated with his body she will find the error of her choice. Therefore put money in your purse. If you will needs damn yourself, do it a more delicate way than drowning. Raise all the money you can. If sanctimony and a frail vow between an erring barbarian and a super-subtle Venetian are not too hard for my wits and all the tribe of hell, you shall enjoy her—therefore raise money. A pox of drowning yourself! It is clean out of the way. Seek you rather to be hanged in compassing your joy than to be drowned and go without her.

RODERIGO Will you be fast to my hopes, if I depend on the issue?

IAGO You are sure of me. Go raise money. I have told you often, and I re-tell you again and again, I hate the Moor. My cause is heart-felt: yours has no less reason. Let us be conjunctive in our revenge against him. If you can cuckold him, you do yourself a pleasure, me a sport. There are many events in the womb of time, which will be delivered. About turn! Go, provide your money. We will have more of this tomorrow. Adieu.

RODERIGO Where shall we meet in the morning?
IAGO At my lodging.
RODERIGO I'll be with you betimes.
IAGO Very well; farewell. Do you hear, Roderigo?
RODERIGO What say you?
IAGO No more of drowning, do you hear?
RODERIGO I am changed.
IAGO Good; farewell. Put money enough in your purse.
RODERIGO I'll sell all my land. *Exit*
IAGO
Thus do I ever make my fool my purse:
For I my own gained knowledge should profane
If I would time expend with such a snipe
But for my sport and profit. I hate the Moor,
And it is thought abroad that between my sheets
He's done my office. I know not if it is true,
But I, for mere suspicion in that kind,
Will do as if for surety. He thinks well of me;
The better shall my purpose work on him.
Cassio's a goodly man: let me see now;
To get his place and to plume up my will
In double knavery. How? How? Let's see.
After some time, to abuse Othello's ear
That he is too familiar with his wife;
He has a person and a smooth disposition
To be suspected, framed to make women false.
The Moor is of a free and open nature,
That thinks men honest that but seem to be so,
And will as tenderly be led by the nose
As asses are.
I have it. It is engendered. Hell and night
Must bring this monstrous birth to the world's light.
Exit

Act II

SCENE I
Cyprus. The port.

Enter Montano and two Gentlemen

MONTANO
What from the cape can you discern at sea?
FIRST GENTLEMAN
Nothing at all; it is a high-wrought flood.
I cannot between the heaven and the main
Descry a sail.
MONTANO
I think the wind does speak aloud at land;
A fuller blast never shook our battlements.
If it has ruffianed so upon the sea,
What ribs of oak, when mountains melt on them,
Can hold the mortise? What shall we hear of this?
SECOND GENTLEMAN
It seems the dispersal of the Turkish fleet:
For do but stand upon the cursing shore,
The chidden billow seems to pelt the clouds;
The wind-shaked surge, with high and monstrous mane,
Seems to cast water on the burning Bear
And quench the guards of the ever-fixèd Pole.
I never did like molestation view
On the angry flood.
MONTANO If the Turkish fleet
Is not sheltered and embayed, they are drowned:
It is impossible they bear it out.

Enter a Gentleman

THIRD GENTLEMAN
News, lads! Our wars are done:
The desperate tempest has so banged the Turks
That their design halts. A ship of Venice
Has seen a grievous wreck and sufferance
On most part of their fleet.

MONTANO
How! Is this true?

THIRD GENTLEMAN The ship is here put in,
A Veronesa; Michael Cassio,
Lieutenant to the warlike Moor, Othello,
Is come on shore; the Moor himself at sea,
And is in full commission here for Cyprus.

MONTANO
I am glad of it: a worthy governor.

THIRD GENTLEMAN
But this same Cassio, though he speaks of comfort
Touching the Turkish loss; yet he looks sadly
And prays the Moor is safe; for they were parted
With foul and violent tempest.

MONTANO Pray heaven he is:
For I have served him, and the man commands
Like a full soldier. Let's to the sea-side, ho!
As well to see the vessel that's come in,
As to throw out our eyes for brave Othello,
Even till we make the main and the aerial blue
An indistinct regard.

THIRD GENTLEMAN Come, let's do so;
For every minute is expectancy
Of more arrivals.

Enter Cassio

CASSIO
Thanks, you the valiant of this warlike isle
That so approve the Moor! O, let the heavens

Give him defence against the elements,
For I have lost him on a dangerous sea.

MONTANO

Is he well shipped?

CASSIO

His bark is stoutly timbered, and his pilot
Of very expert and approved allowance;
Therefore my hopes, not surfeited to death,
Stand in bold shape.

(*Cry within* 'A sail, a sail, a sail!')

CASSIO

What noise?

FOURTH GENTLEMAN

The town is empty; on the brow of the sea
Stand ranks of people, and they cry 'A sail!'

CASSIO

My hopes do shape him for the Governor.

Salvo

SECOND GENTLEMAN

They do discharge their shot of courtesy:
Our friends at least.

CASSIO I pray you, sir, go forth,
And give us truth who 'tis that is arrived.

SECOND GENTLEMAN

I shall. *Exit*

MONTANO

But, good Lieutenant, is your General wived?

CASSIO

Most fortunately: he has achieved a maid
That paragons description and wild fame;
One that excels the quirks of blazoning pens,
And in the essential vesture of creation
Does tire the inventor.

Enter Second Gentleman

How now? Who has put in?

SECOND GENTLEMAN

'Tis one Iago, Ensign to the General.

CASSIO

He's had most favourable and happy speed:
Tempests themselves, high seas, and howling winds,
The guttered rocks and congregated sands,
Traitors enscarped to clog the guiltless keel,
As having sense of beauty, do omit
Their mortal natures, letting go safely by
The divine Desdemona.

MONTANO What is she?

CASSIO

She that I spake of, our great Captain's Captain,
Left in the conduct of the bold Iago,
Whose footing here anticipates our thoughts
A sevennight's speed. Great Jove, Othello guard,
And swell his sail with your own powerful breath,
That he may bless this bay with his tall ship,
Make love's quick pants in Desdemona's arms,
Give renewed fire to our extinguished spirits,
And bring all Cyprus comfort.

Enter Desdemona, Emilia, Iago, Roderigo, and attendants

O, behold,
The riches of the ship are come on shore!
You men of Cyprus, let her have your knees.
Hail to you, lady! And the grace of heaven,
Before, behind you, and on every hand,
Enwheel you round.

DESDEMONA I thank you, valiant Cassio.
What tidings can you tell me of my lord?

CASSIO
He has not yet arrived; nor know I aught
But that he's well, and will be shortly here.
DESDEMONA
O, but I fear! How lost you company?
CASSIO
The great contention of the sea and skies
Parted our fellowship.
(*Cry within*) 'A sail, a sail!'
But hark, a sail!
GENTLEMAN
They give their greeting to the citadel:
This likewise is a friend.
CASSIO See for the news.
Good Ensign, you are welcome. Welcome, mistress.
Let it not gall your patience, good Iago,
That I extend my manners. 'Tis my breeding
That gives me this bold show of courtesy.

He kisses Emilia

IAGO
Sir, would she give you so much of her lips
As of her tongue she oft bestows on me,
You would have enough.
DESDEMONA
Alas, she has no speech.
IAGO In faith, too much.
I find it ever when I have wish to sleep.
However, before your ladyship, I grant
She puts her tongue a little in her heart
And chides with thinking.
EMILIA You have little cause to say so.
IAGO Come on, come on: you are pictures out of doors, bells in your parlours, wild-cats in your kitchens, saints

in your injuries, devils being offended, players in your housewifery, and housewives in your beds.

DESDEMONA
O, fie upon you, slanderer!

IAGO
Nay, it is true, or else I am a Turk:
You rise to play and go to bed to work.

EMILIA
You shall not write my praise.

IAGO
No, let me not.

DESDEMONA
What would you write of me, if you should praise me?

IAGO
O, gentle lady, do not put me to it,
For I am nothing if not critical.

DESDEMONA
Come on, try. There's one gone to the harbour?

IAGO
Ay, madam.

DESDEMONA
(*aside*) I am not merry, but I do beguile
The thing I am by seeming otherwise.
Come, how would you praise me?

IAGO
I am about it, but indeed my invention
Comes from my pate as birdlime does from frieze—
It plucks out brains and all. But my muse labours,
And thus she is delivered.
If she is fair and wise, fairness and wit,
The one is for use, the other uses it.

DESDEMONA
Well praised! How if she is black and witty?

IAGO
If she is black, and thereto has a wit,
She'll find a white that shall her blackness fit.

DESDEMONA
Worse and worse.

EMILIA How if fair and foolish?

IAGO
She never yet was foolish that was fair,
For even her folly helped her to an heir.

DESDEMONA These are old fond paradoxes to make fools laugh in the alehouse. What miserable praise have you for her that's foul and foolish?

IAGO
There's none so foul and foolish thereunto,
But does foul pranks which fair and wise ones do.

DESDEMONA O heavy ignorance! You praise the worst best. But what praise could you bestow on a deserving woman indeed? One that in the authority of her merit did justly put on the proof of very malice itself?

IAGO
She that was ever fair and never proud,
Had tongue at will, and yet was never loud;
Never lacked gold, and yet went never gay;
Fled from her wish, and yet said 'Now I may';
She that being angered, her revenge being nigh,
Bade her wrong wait, and her displeasure fly;
She that in wisdom never was so frail
To change the cod's head for the salmon's tail;
She that could think and never disclose her mind:
See suitors following and not look behind:
She was a one, if ever such one were—

DESDEMONA
To do what?

IAGO
To suckle fools and chronicle small beer.

DESDEMONA
O, most lame and impotent conclusion!
Do not learn of him, Emilia, though he is your husband.

How say you, Cassio, is he not a most profane and liberal counsellor?

CASSIO He speaks home, madam; you may relish him more in the soldier than in the scholar.

IAGO *(aside)* He takes her by the palm. Ay, well said, whisper. With as little a web as this will I ensnare as great a fly as Cassio. Ay, smile upon her, do. I will fetter you in your own courtship. You say true, it is so indeed. If such tricks as these strip you out of your lieutenantry, it had been better you had not kissed your three fingers so oft, which now again you are most apt to play the sir in. Very good: well kissed, an excellent courtesy! It is so indeed. Yet again your fingers to your lips? Would they were screw-pipes for your sake!

Trumpet

(aloud) The Moor! I know his trumpet.

CASSIO 'Tis truly so.

DESDEMONA

Let's meet him and receive him.

CASSIO Lo, where he comes!

Enter Othello and attendants

OTHELLO

O, my fair warrior!

DESDEMONA My dear Othello!

OTHELLO

It gives me wonder great as my content
To see you here before me. O, my soul's joy!
If after every tempest come such calms,
May the winds blow till they have wakened death;
And let the labouring bark climb hills of seas,
Olympus-high, and duck again as low
As hell's from heaven. If it were now to die,

It were now to be most happy; for I fear
My soul has her content so absolute
That not another comfort like to this
Succeeds in unknown fate.

DESDEMONA The heavens forbid
But that our loves and comforts should increase,
Even as our days do grow.

OTHELLO Amen to that, sweet Powers!
I cannot speak enough of this content;
It stops me here; it is too much of joy.

They kiss

And this, and this the greatest discords be
That ever our hearts shall make.

IAGO (*aside*) O, you are well tuned now!
But I'll lower the pegs that make this music,
As honest as I am.

OTHELLO Come, let's to the castle.
News, friends; our wars are done; the Turks are drowned.
How do my old acquaintance of this isle?
Honey, you shall be well desired in Cyprus:
I have found great love among them. O my sweet,
I prattle out of fashion and I dote
In my own comforts. I pray you, good Iago,
Go to the bay and disembark my coffers;
Bring you the Master to the citadel;
He is a good one, and his worthiness
Does challenge much respect. Come, Desdemona,
Once more well met at Cyprus!

Exeunt all except Iago and Roderigo

IAGO (*to soldiers, who go off*) Do you meet me presently at the harbour. (*To Roderigo*) Come hither. If you are valiant—as they say base men being in love have then a nobility in their natures more than is native to them—listen to me. The Lieutenant tonight watches on the court of guard. First, I must tell you this: Desdemona is directly in love with him.

RODERIGO With him? Why, 'tis not possible!

IAGO Lay your finger thus, and let your soul be instructed. Mark me with what violence she first loved the Moor, but for bragging and telling her fantastical lies. And will she love him still for prating? Let not your discreet heart think it. Her eye must be fed. And what delight shall she have to look on the devil? When the blood is made dull with the act of sport, there should be, again to inflame it and give satiety a fresh appetite, loveliness in favour, sympathy in years, manners and beauties: all which the Moor is defective in. Now for want of these required conveniences, her delicate tenderness will find itself abused, begin to heave the gorge, disrelish and abhor the Moor. Very nature will instruct her in it and compel her to some second choice. Now, sir, this granted—as it is a most obvious and unforced position—who stands so eminently in the degree of this fortune as Cassio does?—A knave very voluble; no further conscionable than in putting on the mere form of civil and humane seeming for the better compassing of his lustful and most hidden loose affection. Why, none; why, none—a slippery and subtle knave, a finder out of occasions; that has an eye that can stamp and counterfeit advantages, though true advantage never presents itself; a devilish knave! Besides, the knave is handsome, young, and has all those requisites in him that folly and green minds look after. A pestilent complete knave; and the woman has found him already.

RODERIGO I cannot believe that in her: she's full of most blessed condition.

IAGO Blessed fig's end! The wine she drinks is made of grapes. If she had been blessed, she would never have loved the Moor. Blessed pudding! Did you not see her fiddle with the palm of his hand? Did you not mark that?

RODERIGO Yes, that I did: but that was but courtesy.

IAGO Lechery, by this hand: an index and obscure prologue to the history of lust and foul thoughts. They met so near with their lips that their breaths embraced together. Villainous thoughts, Roderigo! When these mutualities so marshal the way, hard at hand comes the master and main exercise, the incorporate conclusion. Pish! But, sir, be you ruled by me. I have brought you from Venice. Watch you tonight: for the command, I'll lay it upon you. Cassio knows you not; I'll not be far from you. Do you find some occasion to anger Cassio, either by speaking too loud, or crabbing his discipline, or from what other course you please, which the time shall more favourably minister.

RODERIGO Well.

IAGO Sir, he's rash and very sudden in anger, and haply with his truncheon may strike at you: provoke him that he may, for even out of that will I cause these of Cyprus to mutiny, whose appeasement shall come into no true taste again but by the displanting of Cassio. So shall you have a shorter journey to your desires by the means I shall then have to prefer them, and the impediment most profitably removed, without which there is no expectation of our prosperity.

RODERIGO I will do this, if you can bring it to any opportunity.

IAGO I warrant you. Meet me by and by at the citadel. I must fetch his necessaries ashore. Farewell.

RODERIGO Adieu. *Exit*

IAGO

That Cassio loves her, I do well believe it:
That she loves him, 'tis apt and of great credit.
The Moor—howbeit that I endure him not—
Is of a constant, loving, noble nature,
And, I dare think, he'll prove to Desdemona
A most dear husband. Now, I do love her too;

Not out of absolute lust—though peradventure
I stand accountable for as great a sin—
But partly led to diet my revenge
For that I do suspect the lusty Moor
Has leaped into my seat: the thought whereof
Does, like a poisonous mineral, gnaw my inwards,
And nothing can, or shall, content my soul
Till I am evened with him, wife for wife.
Or failing so, yet that I put the Moor
At least into a jealousy so strong
That judgement cannot cure. Which thing to do
If this poor trash of Venice, whom I track
For his quick hunting, responds to incitement,
I'll have our Michael Cassio on the hip,
Abuse him to the Moor in the rank garb—
For I fear Cassio with my night-cap too—
Make the Moor thank me, love me, and reward me
For making him egregiously an ass,
And practising upon his peace and quiet,
Even to madness. 'Tis here, but yet confused:
Knavery's plain face is never seen till used. *Exit*

SCENE II
Cyprus. A street.

Enter Herald, with a proclamation

HERALD It is Othello's pleasure, our noble and valiant General, that upon certain tidings now arrived importing the mere perdition of the Turkish fleet, every man puts himself into triumph: some to dance, some to make bonfires, each man to what sport and revels his addiction leads him. For, besides these beneficial news, it is the celebration of his nuptials. So much was his pleasure should be proclaimed. All stores are open, and there is full liberty of feasting from this present hour of five till the bell has told eleven. Heaven bless the isle of Cyprus and our noble General Othello! *Exit*

SCENE III
The citadel.

Enter Othello, Desdemona, Cassio, and attendants

OTHELLO
Good Michael, look you to the guard tonight.
Let's teach ourselves that honourable stop,
Not to outsport discretion.

CASSIO
Iago has direction what to do;
But, notwithstanding, with my personal eye
Will I look to it.

OTHELLO Iago is most honest.
Michael, good night. Tomorrow with your earliest
Let me have speech with you. (*To Desdemona*) Come, my dear love,
The purchase made, the fruits are to ensue:
That profit's yet to come between me and you.
Good night.
Exeunt Othello, Desdemona, and attendants

Enter Iago

CASSIO Welcome, Iago; we must to the watch.

IAGO Not this hour, Lieutenant; 'tis not yet ten o'clock. Our General cast us thus early for the love of his Desdemona; whom let us not therefore blame. He has not yet made wanton the night with her; and she is sport for Jove.

CASSIO She is a most exquisite lady.

IAGO And, I'll warrant her, full of game.

CASSIO Indeed, she is a most fresh and delicate creature.

IAGO What an eye she has! I think it sounds a parley to provocation.

CASSIO An inviting eye, and yet I think right modest.

IAGO And when she speaks, is it not an alarum to love?

CASSIO She is indeed perfection.

IAGO Well, happiness to their sheets! Come, Lieutenant, I have a stoup of wine; and here without are a brace of Cyprus gallants that would gladly have a measure to the health of black Othello.

CASSIO Not tonight, good Iago. I have very poor and unhappy brains for drinking. I could well wish courtesy would invent some other custom of entertainment.

IAGO O, they are our friends! But one cup; I'll drink for you.

CASSIO I have drunk but one cup tonight, and that was well watered too; and behold what innovation it makes here. I am unfortunate in the infirmity and dare not tax my weakness with any more.

IAGO What, man! 'Tis a night of revels; the gallants desire it.

CASSIO Where are they?

IAGO Here, at the door: I pray you call them in.

CASSIO I'll do it, but it dislikes me. *Exit*

IAGO

If I can fasten but one cup upon him,
With that which he has drunk tonight already,
He'll be as full of quarrel and offence
As my young mistress' dog. Now my sick fool Roderigo,
Whom love has turned almost the wrong side out,
To Desdemona has tonight caroused
Potations bottle-deep; and he's to watch.
Three else of Cyprus, noble swelling spirits—
That hold their honours in a wary distance,
The very elements of this warlike isle—

Have I tonight flustered with flowing cups,
And they watch too. Among this flock of drunkards,
Am I to put our Cassio in some action
That may offend the isle. But here they come;
If consequence does but approve my dream,
My boat sails freely both with wind and stream.

Enter Cassio with Montano and Gentlemen, and servants with wine

CASSIO Before God, they have given me a rouse already.
MONTANO Good faith, a little one; not past a pint, as I am a soldier.
IAGO Some wine, ho!
(*sings*) And let me the canakin clink, clink;
And let me the canakin clink;
A soldier's a man
O, man's life's but a span;
Why, then, let a soldier drink.
Some wine, boys.
CASSIO Before God, an excellent song.
IAGO I learned it in England, where indeed they are most potent in potting. Your Dane, your German, and your swag-bellied Hollander—drink, ho!—are nothing to your English.
CASSIO Is your Englishman so expert in his drinking?
IAGO Why, he drinks with facility your Dane dead drunk; he sweats not to overthrow your German; he gives your Hollander a vomit, ere the next bottle can be filled.
CASSIO To the health of our General!
MONTANO I am for it, Lieutenant; and I'll do you justice.

IAGO O, sweet England!

(*sings*) King Stephen was and-a worthy peer,
His breeches cost him but a crown;
He held them sixpence all too dear;
With that he called the tailor lown.
He was a wight of high renown,
And you are but of low degree;
'Tis pride that pulls the country down;
Then take your auld cloak about thee.

Some wine, ho!

CASSIO Before God, this is a more exquisite song than the other.

IAGO Will you hear it again?

CASSIO No, for I hold him to be unworthy of his place that does those things. Well, God's above all; and there are souls must be saved, and there are souls must not be saved.

IAGO It's true, good Lieutenant.

CASSIO For my own part—no offence to the General, nor any man of quality—I hope to be saved.

IAGO And so do I too, Lieutenant.

CASSIO Ay, but, by your leave, not before me. The Lieutenant is to be saved before the Ensign. Let's have no more of this; let's to our affairs. God forgive us our sins. Gentlemen, let's look to our business. Do not think, gentlemen, I am drunk: this is my Ensign, this is my right hand, and this is my left. I am not drunk now: I can stand well enough and I speak well enough.

GENTLEMEN Excellent well.

CASSIO Why, very well; you must not think then that I am drunk. *Exit*

MONTANO To the platform, masters; come, let's set the watch.

IAGO

You see this fellow that is gone before:
He is a soldier, fit to stand by Caesar

And give direction; and do but see his vice:
It is to his virtue a just equinox,
The one as long as the other. 'Tis pity of him.
I fear the trust Othello puts in him,
On some odd time of his infirmity,
Will shake this island.

MONTANO But is he often thus?

IAGO
It is evermore the prologue to his sleep:
He'll watch the horologe a double set,
If drink rocks not his cradle.

MONTANO It were well
The General were put in mind of it:
Perhaps he sees it not, or his good nature
Prizes the virtue that appears in Cassio
And looks not on his evils. Is not this true?

Enter Roderigo

IAGO
(*aside*) How now, Roderigo!
I pray you after the Lieutenant go! *Exit Roderigo*

MONTANO
It is great pity that the noble Moor
Should hazard such a place as his own second
With one of an ingrafted infirmity.
It were an honest action to say
So to the Moor.

IAGO Not I, for this fair island!
I do love Cassio well and would do much
To cure him of this evil.
(*Cry within*) 'Help! Help!'
But hark, what noise?
Enter Cassio, pursuing Roderigo

CASSIO Zounds, you rogue, you rascal!

MONTANO What's the matter, Lieutenant?

CASSIO A knave teach me my duty? I'll beat the knave into a wicker-bottle.

RODERIGO Beat me?

CASSIO Do you prate, rogue?

He strikes Roderigo

MONTANO Nay, good Lieutenant; I pray you, sir, hold your hand.

CASSIO Let me go, sir, or I'll knock you over the nut.

MONTANO Come, come, you're drunk.

CASSIO Drunk!

IAGO (*to Roderigo*) Away, I say; go out and cry a mutiny.

Exit Roderigo

Nay, good Lieutenant. God's will, gentleman!
Help, ho! Lieutenant! Sir! Montano! Sir!
Help, masters. Here's a goodly watch indeed.

Bell rings

Who's that who rings the bell? Diablo, ho!
The town will rise. God's will, Lieutenant, hold!
You will be shamed for ever!

Enter Othello and attendants

OTHELLO
What is the matter here?

MONTANO Zounds, I bleed still.
I am hurt to the death.

OTHELLO Hold for your lives!

IAGO
Hold, ho, Lieutenant, sir, Montano, gentlemen!
Have you forgotten all sense of place and duty?
Hold! The General speaks to you: hold, for shame!

OTHELLO

Why, how now, ho! From whence arises this?
Are we turned Turks and to ourselves do that
Which heaven has forbidden the Ottomites?
For Christian shame, put by this barbarous brawl.
He that stirs next to carve for his own rage
Holds his soul light: he dies upon his motion.
Silence that dreadful bell: it frightens the isle
From its propriety. What is the matter, masters?
Honest Iago, that looks dead with grieving,
Speak, who began this? On your love I charge you.

IAGO

I do not know. Friends all but now, even now,
In quarter and in terms like bride and groom
Divesting them for bed. And then but now—
As if some planet had unwitted men—
Swords out, and tilting one at others' breasts
In opposition bloody. I cannot speak
Any beginning to this peevish odds;
And would in action glorious I had lost
Those legs that brought me to a part of it.

OTHELLO

How comes it, Michael, you are thus forgotten?

CASSIO

I pray you pardon me: I cannot speak.

OTHELLO

Worthy Montano, you were wont to be civil:
The gravity and stillness of your youth
The world has noted; and your name is great
In mouths of wisest judgement. What's the matter
That you unlace your reputation thus
And spend your good standing for the name
Of a night-brawler? Give me answer to it.

MONTANO

Worthy Othello, I am hurt to danger.
Your officer, Iago, can inform you,

While I spare speech, which somewhat now offends me,
Of all that I do know; nor know I aught
By me that's said or done amiss this night,
Unless self-charity be sometimes a vice,
And to defend ourselves it is a sin
When violence assails us.

OTHELLO Now, by heaven,
My blood begins my safer guides to rule,
And passion, having my best judgement darkened,
Attempts to lead the way. Zounds, if I stir,
Or do but lift this arm, the best of you
Shall sink in my rebuke. Give me to know
How this foul rout began, who set it on;
And he that is proved guilty in this offence,
Though he had twinned with me, both at a birth,
Shall lose me. What! In a town of war
Yet wild, the people's hearts brimful of fear,
To manage private and domestic quarrel
At night, and on the court and guard of safety,
It is monstrous. Iago, who began it?

MONTANO
If partially allied or leagued in office,
You do deliver more or less than truth,
You are no soldier.

IAGO Touch me not so near.
I had rather have this tongue cut from my mouth
Than it should do offence to Michael Cassio.
Yet, I persuade myself, to speak the truth
Shall nothing wrong him. This it is, General.
Montano and myself being in speech,
There comes a fellow, crying out for help,
And Cassio following with determined sword
To execute upon him. Sir, this gentleman
Steps in to Cassio and entreats his pause:
Myself the crying fellow did pursue
Lest by his clamour—as it so fell out—

The town might fall in fright. He, swift of foot,
Outran my purpose and I returned the rather
For that I heard the clink and fall of swords
And Cassio high in oath, which till tonight
I never might say before. When I came back—
For this was brief—I found them close together
At blow and thrust, even as again they were
When you yourself did part them.
More of this matter can I not report:
But men are men; the best sometimes forget.
Though Cassio did some little wrong to him,
As men in rage strike those that wish them best,
Yet surely Cassio, I believe, received
From him that fled some strange indignity
Which patience could not pass.

OTHELLO I know, Iago,
Your honesty and love do mince this matter,
Making it light to Cassio. Cassio, I love you
But nevermore be officer of mine.

Enter Desdemona, attended

Look, if my gentle love be not raised up.
I'll make you an example.

DESDEMONA What is the matter, dear?

OTHELLO
All's well now, sweeting: come away to bed.
Sir, for your hurts myself will be your surgeon.
Montano is led off
Iago, look with care about the town
And silence those whom this vile brawl distracted.
Come, Desdemona, it is the soldiers' life
To have their balmy slumbers waked with strife.
Exeunt all but Iago and Cassio

IAGO What, are you hurt, Lieutenant?

CASSIO Ay, past all surgery.

IAGO God forbid!

CASSIO Reputation, reputation, reputation! O, I have lost my reputation! I have lost the immortal part of myself, and what remains is bestial. My reputation, Iago, my reputation!

IAGO As I am an honest man I thought you had received some bodily wound: there is more of sense in that than in reputation. Reputation is an idle and most false imposition; often got without merit and lost without deserving. You have lost no reputation at all, unless you repute yourself such a loser. What, man! There are ways to recover the General again. You are but now sack in his mood—a punishment more in policy than in malice—even so as one would beat his offenceless dog to affright an imperious lion. Sue to him again, and he's yours.

CASSIO I will rather sue to be despised than to deceive so good a commander with so slight, so drunken, and so indiscreet an officer. Drunk! And speak parrot! And squabble! Swagger! Swear! And discourse fustian with one's own shadow! O, you invisible spirit of wine, if you have no name to be known by, let us call you devil.

IAGO What was he that you followed with your sword? What had he done to you?

CASSIO I know not.

IAGO Is it possible?

CASSIO I remember a mass of things, but nothing distinctly: a quarrel, but nothing wherefore. O God, that men should put an enemy in their mouths to steal away their brains! That we should with joy, pleasure, revel and applause transform ourselves into beasts!

IAGO Why, but you are now well enough! How came you thus recovered?

CASSIO It has pleased the devil drunkenness to give place to the devil wrath: one unperfectness shows me another, to make me frankly despise myself.

IAGO Come, you are too severe a moralist. As the time, the place and the condition of this country stand, I could heartily wish this had not so befallen: but since it is as it is, mend it for your own good.

CASSIO I will ask him for my place again; he shall tell me I am a drunkard. Had I as many mouths as Hydra, such an answer would stop them all. To be now a sensible man, by and by a fool, and presently a beast! O, strange! Every inordinate cup is unblessed and the ingredients a devil.

IAGO Come, come; good wine is a good familiar creature if it is well used: exclaim no more against it. And, good Lieutenant, I think you think I love you.

CASSIO I have well proved it, sir. I drunk!

IAGO You or any man living may be drunk at a time, man. I'll tell you what you shall do. Our General's wife is now the General. I may say so in this respect, for he has devoted and given up himself to the contemplation, mark, and denotement of her parts and graces. Confess yourself freely to her; importune her help to put you in your place again. She is of so free, so kind, so apt, so blessed a disposition, that she holds it a vice in her goodness not to do more than she is requested. This broken joint between you and her husband, entreat her to put in a splint; and my fortunes against any lay worth naming, this crack of your love shall grow stronger than it was before.

CASSIO You advise me well.

IAGO I protest in the sincerity of love and honest kindness.

CASSIO I think it freely; and betimes in the morning I will beseech the virtuous Desdemona to undertake for me. I am desperate of my fortunes if they check me here.

IAGO You are in the right. Good night, Lieutenant, I must to the watch.

CASSIO Good night, honest Iago. *Exit*

IAGO

And what's he then that says I play the villain,
When this advice is free I give, and honest,

Proven to thinking, and indeed the course
To win the Moor again? For it is most easy
The inclining Desdemona to subdue
In any honest suit. She's framed as fruitful
As the free elements; and then for her
To win the Moor, were it to renounce his baptism,
All seals and symbols of redeemèd sin,
His soul is so enfettered to her love,
That she may make, unmake, do what she likes,
Even as her appetite shall play the god
With his weak function. How am I then a villain
To counsel Cassio to this parallel course
Directly to his good? Divinity of hell!
When devils will the blackest sins put on,
They do suggest at first with heavenly shows
As I do now. For while this honest fool
Plies Desdemona to repair his fortunes,
And she for him pleads strongly to the Moor,
I'll pour this pestilence into his ear:
That she affects him for her body's lust,
And by how much she strives to do him good,
She shall undo her credit with the Moor.
So will I turn her virtue into pitch,
And out of her own goodness make the net
That shall enmesh them all.

Enter Roderigo

How now, Roderigo?

RODERIGO I do follow here in the chase, not like a hound that hunts, but one that fills up the cry. My money is almost spent; I have been tonight exceedingly well cudgelled; and I think the issue will be, I shall have so much experience for my pains; and so, with no money at all, and a little more wit, return again to Venice.

IAGO

How poor are they that have not patiènce!
What wound did ever heal but by degrees?
You know we work by wit, and not by witchcraft,
And wit depends on dilatory time.
Does it not go well? Cassio has beaten you,
And you by that small hurt have cashiered Cassio.
Though other things grow fair against the sun,
Yet fruits that blossom first will first be ripe.
Content yourself awhile. By the mass, 'tis morning:
Pleasure and action make the hours seem short.
Retire you; go where you are billeted.
Away, I say, you shall know more hereafter:
Nay, get you gone. *Exit Roderigo*
Two things are to be done.
My wife must move for Cassio to her mistress:
I'll set her on.
Myself the while to draw the Moor apart,
And bring him just when he may Cassio find
Soliciting his wife. Ay, that's the way.
Dull not device by coldness and delay. *Exit*

Act III

SCENE I
Before the citadel.

Enter Cassio and Musicians

CASSIO
Masters, play here—I will content your pains—
Something that's brief; and bid 'Good morrow, General'.

They play
Enter Clown

CLOWN Why, masters, have your instruments been in Naples, that they speak in the nose thus?

FIRST MUSICIAN How, sir, how?

CLOWN Are these, I pray you, wind instruments?

FIRST MUSICIAN Ay, indeed are they, sir.

CLOWN O, thereby hangs a tail.

FIRST MUSICIAN Whereby hangs a tale, sir?

CLOWN Sure, sir, by many a wind instrument that I know. But, masters, here's money for you: and the General so likes your music that he desires you, for love's sake, to make no more noise with it.

FIRST MUSICIAN Well, sir, we will not.

CLOWN If you have any music that may not be heard, to it again. But, as they say, to hear music the General does not greatly care.

FIRST MUSICIAN We have none such, sir.

CLOWN Then put up your pipes in your bag, for I'll away. Go, vanish into air, away. *Exeunt Musicians*

CASSIO Do you hear, my honest friend?

CLOWN No, I hear not your honest friend: I hear you.

CASSIO Pray keep up your quibbles—there's a poor piece of gold for you. If the gentlewoman that attends the General's wife is stirring, tell her there's one Cassio entreats her a little favour of speech. Will you do this?

CLOWN She is stirring, sir. If she will stir hither, I shall seem to notify unto her.

CASSIO Do, good my friend. *Exit Clown*

Enter Iago

In happy time, Iago.

IAGO You have not been abed then?

CASSIO
Why, no: the day had broken before we parted.
I have made bold, Iago,
To send in to your wife. My suit to her
Is that she will to virtuous Desdemona
Procure me some access.

IAGO I'll send her to you at once;
And I'll devise a means to draw the Moor
Out of the way, that your converse and business
May be more free.

CASSIO I humbly thank you for it.

Exit Iago

I never knew a Florentine more kind and honest.

Enter Emilia

EMILIA
Good morrow, good Lieutenant; I am sorry
For your displeasure: but all will sure be well.
The General and his wife are talking of it,
And she speaks for you stoutly. The Moor replies
That he you hurt is of great fame in Cyprus,

And great affinity; and that in wholesome wisdom
He might not but refuse you. But he protests he loves
you
And needs no other suitor but his likings
To take the safest occasion by the front
To bring you in again.

CASSIO Yet I beseech you,
If you think fit, or that it may be done,
Give me advantage of some brief discourse
With Desdemona alone.

EMILIA Pray you, come in:
I will bestow you where you shall have time
To speak your bosom freely.

CASSIO I am much bound to you.

Exeunt

SCENE II
The citadel.

Enter Othello, Iago, and Gentlemen

OTHELLO
These letters give, Iago, to the pilot,
And by him do my duties to the senate.
That done, I will be walking on the works:
Repair there to me.

IAGO Well, my good lord, I'll do it. *Exit*

OTHELLO
This fortification, gentlemen, shall we see it?

GENTLEMEN
We'll wait upon your lordship. *Exeunt*

SCENE III
The same.

Enter Desdemona, Cassio, and Emilia

DESDEMONA
Be you assured, good Cassio, I will do
All my abilities in your behalf.

EMILIA
Good madam, do: I warrant it grieves my husband
As if the case were his.

DESDEMONA
O, that's an honest fellow! Do not doubt, Cassio,
But I will have my lord and you again
As friendly as you were.

CASSIO Bounteous madam,
Whatever shall become of Michael Cassio,
He's never anything but your true servant.

DESDEMONA
I know it: I thank you. You do love my lord;
You have known him long, and be you well assured
He shall in strangeness stand no farther off
Than in a politic distance.

CASSIO Ay, but, lady,
That policy may either last so long,
Or feed upon such nice and waterish diet,
Or breed itself so out of circumstance,
That I being absent and my place supplied,
My General will forget my love and service.

DESDEMONA
Do not doubt that. Before Emilia here,
I give you warrant of your place. Assure you,
If I do vow a friendship, I will perform it
To the last article. My lord shall never rest.
I'll watch him tame and talk him out of patience;
His bed shall seem a school, his board a shrift;

I'll intermingle everything he does
With Cassio's suit. Therefore be merry, Cassio,
For your solicitor shall rather die
Than give your cause away.

Enter Othello and Iago

EMILIA
Madam, here comes my lord.

CASSIO
Madam, I'll take my leave.

DESDEMONA
Why, stay and hear me speak.

CASSIO
Madam, not now: I am very ill at ease,
Unfit for my own purposes.

DESDEMONA
Well, do your discretion. *Exit Cassio*

IAGO
Ha! I like not that.

OTHELLO What do you say?

IAGO
Nothing, my lord; or if—I know not what.

OTHELLO
Was not that Cassio parted from my wife?

IAGO
Cassio, my lord? No, sure, I cannot think it
That he would sneak away so guilty-like,
Seeing you coming.

OTHELLO I do believe it was he.

DESDEMONA
How now, my lord?
I have been talking with a suitor here,
A man that languishes in your displeasure.

OTHELLO
Who is it you mean?

DESDEMONA
Why, your Lieutenant, Cassio. Good my lord,
If I have any grace or power to move you,
His present reconciliation take.
For if he is not one that truly loves you,
That errs in ignorance, and not in cunning,
I have no judgement in an honest face.
I pray you call him back.

OTHELLO Went he hence now?

DESDEMONA
Yes, faith; so humbled
That he has left part of his grief with me
To suffer with him. Good love, call him back.

OTHELLO
Not now, sweet Desdemon; some other time.

DESDEMONA
But shall it be shortly?

OTHELLO The sooner, sweet, for you.

DESDEMONA
Shall it be tonight, at supper?

OTHELLO No, not tonight.

DESDEMONA
Tomorrow dinner then?

OTHELLO I shall not dine at home.
I meet the captains at the citadel.

DESDEMONA
Why, then, tomorrow night, or Tuesday morn,
On Tuesday noon, or night; on Wednesday morn.
Pray you name the time, but let it not
Exceed three days. In faith, he is penitent:
And yet his trespass in our common reason—
Save that, they say, the wars must make example
Out of their best—is not almost a fault
To incur a private check. When shall he come?
Tell me, Othello. I wonder in my soul
What you would ask me that I should deny,

Or stand so stammering on? What! Michael Cassio,
That came a-wooing with you? And so many a time—
When I have spoken of you dispraisingly—
Has taken your part, to have so much to do
To bring him in? By our Lady, I could do much.

OTHELLO
Pray you, no more: let him come when he will;
I will deny you nothing.

DESDEMONA Why, this is not a boon:
'Tis as I should entreat you wear your gloves
Or feed on nourishing dishes, or keep you warm;
Or sue to you to do a peculiar profit
To your own person. Nay, when I have a suit
Wherein I mean to touch your love indeed
It shall be full of poise and difficult weight,
And fearful to be granted.

OTHELLO I will deny you nothing.
Whereon, I do beseech you, grant me this:
To leave me but a little to my self.

DESDEMONA
Shall I deny you? No; farewell, my lord.

OTHELLO
Farewell, my Desdemona, I'll come to you straight.

DESDEMONA
Emilia, come. Be as your fancies teach you.
Whatever you are, I am obedient.

Exeunt Desdemona and Emilia

OTHELLO
Excellent wench! Perdition catch my soul
But I do love you! And when I love you not,
Chaos is come again.

IAGO My noble lord—

OTHELLO
What do you say, Iago?

IAGO Did Michael Cassio,
When you wooed my lady, know of your love?

OTHELLO
He did, from first to last. Why do you ask?
IAGO
But for a satisfaction of my thought—
No further harm.
OTHELLO Why of your thought, Iago?
IAGO
I did not think he had been acquainted with her.
OTHELLO
O yes, and went between us very often.
IAGO
Indeed!
OTHELLO
Indeed? Ay, indeed. Discern you aught in that?
Is he not honest?
IAGO Honest, my lord?
OTHELLO Honest? Ay, honest.
IAGO
My lord, for aught I know.
OTHELLO What do you think?
IAGO
Think, my lord?
OTHELLO
Think, my lord! By heaven, he echoes me,
As if there were some monster in his thought
Too hideous to be shown. You do mean something.
I heard you say even now, you like not that,
When Cassio left my wife. What did you not like?
And when I told you he was of my counsel
In my whole course of wooing, you cried 'Indeed!'
And did contract and purse your brow together,
As if you then had shut up in your brain
Some horrible idea. If you do love me,
Show me your thought.
IAGO
My lord, you know I love you.

OTHELLO I think you do:
Because I know you are full of love and honesty,
And weigh your words before you give them breath,
Therefore these stops of yours affright me more.
For such things in a false disloyal knave
Are tricks of custom; but in a man that's just,
They're close dilations, working from the heart,
That passion cannot rule.

IAGO For Michael Cassio,
I dare be sworn I think that he is honest.

OTHELLO
I think so too.

IAGO Men should be what they seem;
Or those that are not, would they might seem none!

OTHELLO
Certain, men should be what they seem.

IAGO
Why, then, I think Cassio's an honest man.

OTHELLO
Nay, yet there's more in this.
I pray speak to me as to your thinkings,
As you do ruminate, and give your worst of thoughts
The worst of words.

IAGO Good my lord, pardon me;
Though I am bound to every act of duty,
I am not bound to that all slaves are free to:
Utter my thoughts. Why, say they are vile and false?
As where's that palace whereinto foul things
Sometimes intrude not? Who has a breast so pure,
But some uncleanly apprehensions
Keep courts and law-days, and in session sit
With meditations lawful?

OTHELLO
You do conspire against your friend, Iago,
If you but think him wronged, and make his ear
A stranger to your thoughts.

IAGO I do beseech you,
Though I perhaps am vicious in my guess—
As I confess it is my nature's plague
To spy into abuses, and of suspicion
Shape faults that are not—that your wisdom then,
From one that so imperfectly conjectures,
Would take no notice, nor build yourself a trouble
Out of his scattering and unsure observance.
It were not for your quiet nor your good,
Nor for my manhood, honesty, and wisdom,
To let you know my thoughts.

OTHELLO What do you mean?

IAGO
Good name in man and woman, dear my lord,
Is the immediate jewel of their souls.
Who steals my purse, steals trash; 'tis something, nothing;
'Twas mine, 'tis his, and has been slave to thousands.
But he that filches from me my good name
Robs me of that which not enriches him
And makes me poor indeed.

OTHELLO By heaven, I'll know your thoughts.

IAGO
You cannot, if my heart were in your hand,
And shall not, while 'tis in my custody.

OTHELLO
Ha!

IAGO O, beware, my lord, of jealousy!
It is the green-eyed monster, which does mock
The meat it feeds on. That cuckold lives in bliss
Who certain of his fate loves not his wronger;
But O, what damnèd minutes tells he over,
Who dotes yet doubts, suspects yet fondly loves!

OTHELLO
O misery!

IAGO
Poor and content is rich, and rich enough;
But riches boundless are as poor as winter,
To him that ever fears he shall be poor.
Good God, the souls of all my tribe defend
From jealousy!
OTHELLO Why, why is this?
Think you I'd make a life of jealousy,
To follow still the changes of the moon
With fresh suspicions? No, to be once in doubt
Is once to be resolved. Exchange me for a goat,
When I shall turn the business of my soul
To such inflated and blown-up surmises,
Matching your inference. 'Tis not to make me jealous
To say my wife is fair, loves company,
Is free of speech, sings, plays, and dances well:
Where virtue is, these are more virtuous.
Nor from my own weak merits will I draw
The smallest fear or suspicion of her change,
For she had eyes and chose me. No, Iago,
I'll see before I doubt; when I doubt, prove;
And on the proof, there is no more but this:
Away at once with love or jealousy!
IAGO
I am glad of this: for now I shall have reason
To show the love and duty that I bear you
With franker spirit. Therefore, as I am bound,
Receive it from me. I speak not yet of proof.
Look to your wife; observe her well with Cassio.
Wear your eye thus: not jealous, nor secure.
I would not have your free and noble nature,
Out of self-bounty, be abused. Look to it.
I know our country disposition well:
In Venice they do let God see the pranks
They dare not show their husbands; their best conscience
Is not to leave it undone, but keep it unknown.

OTHELLO
Do you say so?
IAGO
She did deceive her father, marrying you,
And when she seemed to shake, and fear your looks,
She loved them most.
OTHELLO And so she did.
IAGO Why, very well then!
She that so young could give out such a seeming,
To sew her father's eyes up close as oak—
He thought it was witchcraft.—But I am much to blame,
I humbly do beseech you of your pardon
For too much loving you.
OTHELLO I am bound to you for ever.
IAGO
I see this has a little dashed your spirits.
OTHELLO
Not a jot, not a jot.
IAGO In faith, I fear it has.
I hope you will consider that what is spoken
Comes from my love. But I do see you are moved.
I am to pray you, not to strain my speech
To grosser issues, nor to larger reach
Than to suspicion.
OTHELLO
I will not.
IAGO Should you do so, my lord,
My speech should fall into such vile result
Which my thoughts aimed not at. Cassio's my worthy friend.
My lord, I see you are moved.
OTHELLO No, not much moved.
I do not think but Desdemona's honest.
IAGO
Long live she so! And long live you to think so!

OTHELLO
And yet, how nature erring from itself—
IAGO
Ay, there's the point: as, to be bold with you,
Not to affect many proposèd matches
Of her own clime, complexion, and degree,
Whereto we see in all things nature tends,
Foh! One may smell in such a will most rank,
Foul disproportion, thoughts unnatural.
But, pardon me, I do not in position
Distinctly speak of her, though I may fear
Her will, recoiling to her better judgement,
May fall to match you with her inborn ways,
And maybe repent.
OTHELLO Farewell, farewell.
If more you do perceive, let me know more.
Set on your wife to observe. Leave me, Iago.
IAGO
(*going*) My lord, I take my leave.
OTHELLO
Why did I marry? This honest creature doubtless
Sees and knows more, much more than he unfolds.
IAGO
(*returning*) My lord, I would I might entreat your honour
To scan this thing no farther. Leave it to time.
Although it is fit that Cassio have his place,
For sure he fills it up with great ability,
Yet, if you please to hold him off awhile,
You shall by that perceive him and his means.
Note if your lady strains his entertainment
With any strong or vehement importunity—
Much will be seen in that. In the meantime,
Let me be thought too busy in my fears,
As worthy cause I have to fear I am,
And hold her free, I do beseech your honour.

OTHELLO
Fear not my government.
IAGO I once more take my leave. *Exit*
OTHELLO
This fellow's of exceeding honesty,
And knows all qualities with a learnèd spirit
Of human dealings. If she proves a wild bird,
Though her ties were my dearest heart-strings,
I'd whistle her off, and let her down the wind
To prey at fortune. Haply, for I am black
And have not those soft parts of conversation
That chamberers have. Or because I am declined
Into the vale of years—yet that's not much—
She's gone: I am abused, and my relief
Must be to loathe her. O, curse of marriage!
That we can call these delicate creatures ours
And not their appetites! I had rather be a toad
And live upon the vapour of a dungeon
Than keep a corner in the thing I love
For others' uses. Yet 'tis the plague of great ones;
Prerogatived are they less than the base.
'Tis destiny unshunnable, like death:
Even then this forkèd plague is fated to us
When we are conceived. Desdemona comes:

Enter Desdemona and Emilia

If she is false, O, then heaven mocks itself!
I'll not believe it.
DESDEMONA How now, my dear Othello!
Your dinner, and the generous islanders
By you invited, do attend your presence.
OTHELLO
I am to blame.
DESDEMONA Why do you speak so faintly?
Are you not well?

OTHELLO
I have a pain upon my forehead here.
DESDEMONA
Faith, that's with watching: 'twill away again.
Let me but bind it hard, within this hour
It will be well.
OTHELLO Your napkin is too little.

He puts the handkerchief from him, and she drops it

Let it alone. Come, I'll go in with you.
DESDEMONA
I am very sorry that you are not well.
Exeunt Othello and Desdemona
EMILIA
I am glad I have found this napkin:
This was her first remembrance from the Moor.
My wayward husband has a hundred times
Wooed me to steal it. But she so loves the token—
For he conjùred her she should ever keep it—
That she reserves it evermore about her
To kiss and talk to. I'll have the work taken out,
And give it Iago.
What he will do with it, heaven knows, not I:
I nothing, but to please his fantasy.

Enter Iago

IAGO
How now? What do you here alone?
EMILIA
Do not you chide: I have a thing for you.
IAGO
A thing for me? It is a common thing.
EMILIA
Ha!

IAGO

To have a foolish wife.

EMILIA

O, is that all? What will you give me now
For that same handkerchief?

IAGO What handkerchief?

EMILIA

What handkerchief!
Why that the Moor first gave to Desdemona;
That which so often you did bid me steal.

IAGO

Have you stolen it from her?

EMILIA

No, faith, she let it drop by negligence,
And to the advantage, I, being here, took it up.
Look, here it is.

IAGO A good wench! Give it me.

EMILIA

What will you do with it, that you have been so earnest
To have me filch it?

IAGO *(snatching it)* Why, what is that to you?

EMILIA

If it is not for some purpose of import,
Give it me again. Poor lady, she'll run mad
When she shall lack it.

IAGO

Acknowledge it not: I have use for it.
Go, leave me. *Exit Emilia*
I will in Cassio's lodging lose this napkin,
And let him find it. Trifles light as air
Are to the jealous confirmations strong
As proofs of holy writ. This may do something.
The Moor already changes with my poison.
Dangerous conceits are in their natures poisons,
Which at the first are scarce found to distaste,

But, with a little act upon the blood,
Burn like the mines of sulphur.

Enter Othello

I did say so.
Look where he comes! Not poppy, nor mandragora,
Nor all the drowsy syrups of the world,
Shall ever medicine you to that sweet sleep
Which you owned yesterday.

OTHELLO Ha, ha, false to me!

IAGO
Why, how now, General! No more of that.

OTHELLO
Away! Be gone! You have set me on the rack.
I swear it is better to be much abused,
Than but to know it a little.

IAGO How now, my lord!

OTHELLO
What sense had I of her stolen hours of lust?
I saw it not, thought it not, it harmed not me.
I slept the next night well, was free and merry;
I found not Cassio's kisses on her lips.
He that is robbed, not wanting what is stolen,
Let him not know it, and he's not robbed at all.

IAGO
I am sorry to hear this.

OTHELLO
I had been happy if the general camp,
Sappers and all, had tasted her sweet body,
So I had nothing known. O, now, for ever
Farewell the tranquil mind! Farewell content!
Farewell the plumèd troops and the big wars
That make ambition virtue—O, farewell!
Farewell the neighing steed, and the shrill trump,
The spirit-stirring drum, the ear-piercing fife,

The royal banner and all quality,
Pride, pomp and circumstance of glorious war!
And, O you mortal engines, whose rude throats
The immortal Jove's dread clamours counterfeit,
Farewell! Othello's occupation's gone.

IAGO

Is it possible, my lord?

OTHELLO

Villain, be sure you prove my love a whore.
Be sure of it: give me the ocular proof,
Or by the worth of my eternal soul,
You had been better have been born a dog
Than answer my waked wrath!

IAGO Is it come to this?

OTHELLO

Make me to see it: or, at the least, so prove it
That the probation bears no hinge or loop
To hang a doubt on—or woe upon your life!

IAGO

My noble lord—

OTHELLO

If you do slander her and torture me,
Never pray more; abandon all remorse;
On horror's head horrors accumulate,
Do deeds to make heaven weep, all earth amazed:
For nothing can you to damnation add
Greater than that.

IAGO O grace! O heaven defend me!
Are you a man? Have you a soul? Or sense?
Goodbye to you: take my office. O wretched fool,
That loves to make your honesty a vice!
O monstrous world! Take note, take note, O world!
To be direct and honest is not safe.
I thank you for this profit, and from hence
I'll love no friend, since love breeds such offence.

OTHELLO
Nay, stay: you should be honest.

IAGO
I should be wise; for honesty's a fool
And loses what it works for.

OTHELLO By the world,
I think my wife is chaste, and think she is not;
I think that you are just, and think you are not.
I'll have some proof. Her name that was as fresh
As Dian's visage is now begrimed and black
As my own face. If there are cords or knives,
Poison or fire or suffocating streams,
I'll not endure it. Would I were satisfied!

IAGO
I see, sir, you are eaten up with passion.
I do repent me that I put it to you.
You would be satisfied?

OTHELLO Would! Nay, I will.

IAGO
And may. But how? How satisfied, my lord?
Would you, the supervisor, grossly gape on?
Behold her topped?

OTHELLO Death and damnation! O!

IAGO
It were a tedious difficulty, I think,
To bring them to that prospect. Damn them then
If ever mortal eyes do see them bolster
More than their own! What then? How then?
What shall I say? Where's satisfactiòn?
It is impossible you should see this,
Were they as prime as goats, as hot as monkeys,
As salt as wolves in pride, and fools as gross
As ignorance made drunk. But yet, I say,
If imputation and strong circumstance,
Which lead directly to the door of truth,
Will give you satisfaction, you might have it.

OTHELLO

Give me a living reason she is disloyal.

IAGO

I do not like the office.
But since I am entered in this cause so far—
Pricked to it by foolish honesty and love—
I will go on. I lay with Cassio lately,
And being troubled with a raging tooth
I could not sleep.
There are a kind of men so loose of soul
That in their sleep will mutter their affairs:
One of this kind is Cassio.
In sleep I heard him say: 'Sweet Desdemona,
Let us be wary, let us hide our loves';
And then, sir, would he grip and wring my hand,
Cry 'O sweet creature!' and then kiss me hard,
As if he plucked up kisses by the roots,
That grew upon my lips. Then laid his leg
Over my thigh, and sighed and kissed, and then
Cried 'Cursèd fate that gave you to the Moor!'

OTHELLO

O monstrous! Monstrous!

IAGO Nay, this was but his dream.

OTHELLO

But this denoted a foregone conclusiòn.

IAGO

It is suspicious, though it is but a dream:
And this may help to thicken other proofs
That do demonstrate thinly.

OTHELLO I'll tear her all to pieces!

IAGO

Nay, but be wise: yet we see nothing done,
She may be honest yet. Tell me but this:
Have you not sometimes seen a handkerchief,
Spotted with strawberries, in your wife's hand?

OTHELLO

I gave her such a one: it was my first gift.

IAGO

I know not that: but such a handkerchief—
I am sure it was your wife's—did I today
See Cassio wipe his beard with.

OTHELLO If it is that—

IAGO

If it is that, or any that was hers,
It speaks against her with the other proofs.

OTHELLO

O, that the slave had forty thousand lives!
One is too poor, too weak for my revenge.
Now do I see it is true. Look here, Iago—
All my fond love thus do I blow to heaven:
It is gone.
Arise, black vengeance, from your hollow cell!
Yield up, O love, your crown and hearted throne
To tyrannous hate! Swell, bosom, with your freight,
For 'tis of serpents' tongues!

IAGO Yet be content.

OTHELLO

O, blood, blood, blood!

IAGO

Patience, I say: your mind perhaps may change.

OTHELLO

Never, Iago. Like to the Pontic sea,
Whose icy current and compulsive course
Never feels retiring ebb, but keeps due on
To the Propontic and the Hellespont.
Even so my bloody thoughts with violent pace
Shall never look back, never ebb to humble love,
Till that a capable and wide revenge
Swallow them up. Now, by yon marble heaven,
In the due reverence of a sacred vow
I here engage my words.

He kneels

IAGO Do not rise yet.

He kneels

Witness you ever-burning lights above,
You elements, that embrace us round about,
Witness that here Iago does give up
The execution of his wit, hands, heart,
To wronged Othello's service. Let him command,
And to obey shall be in me compassion,
What bloody business ever.

They rise

OTHELLO I greet your love,
Not with vain thanks, but with acceptance bounteous;
And will upon the instant put you to it.
Within these three days let me hear you say
That Cassio's not alive.

IAGO My friend is dead;
It is done at your request. But let her live.

OTHELLO
Damn her, lewd minx! O, damn her, damn her!
Come go with me apart. I will withdraw
To furnish me with some swift means of death
For the fair devil. Now are you my Lieutenant.

IAGO
I am your own for ever. *Exeunt*

SCENE IV
The same.

Enter Desdemona, Emilia, and Clown

DESDEMONA Do you know, fellow, where Lieutenant Cassio lies?

CLOWN I dare not say he lies anywhere.

DESDEMONA Why, man?

CLOWN He's a soldier, and for one to say a soldier lies is stabbing.

DESDEMONA Very well, where lodges he?

CLOWN To tell you where he lodges is to tell you where I lie.

DESDEMONA Can anything be made of this?

CLOWN I know not where he lodges, and for me to devise a lodging, and say he lies here, or he lies there, were to lie in my own throat.

DESDEMONA Can you inquire him out? And be edified by report?

CLOWN I will catechize the world for him, that is, make questions, and by them answer.

DESDEMONA Seek him; bid him come hither; tell him I have moved my lord on his behalf, and hope all will be well.

CLOWN To do this is within the compass of man's wit, and therefore I will attempt the doing of it. *Exit*

DESDEMONA
Where should I lose that handkerchief, Emilia?

EMILIA
I know not, madam.

DESDEMONA
Believe me, I had rather have lost my purse
Full of florins; and, but that my noble Moor
Is true of mind, and made of no such baseness
As jealous creatures are, it were enough
To put him to ill-thinking.

EMILIA Is he not jealous?

DESDEMONA
Who? He? I think the sun where he was born
Drew all such humours from him.
EMILIA Look where he comes.

Enter Othello

DESDEMONA
I will not leave him now till Cassio
Is called to him. How is it with you, my lord?
OTHELLO
Well, my good lady. (*Aside*) O, hardness to dissemble!
How do you, Desdemona?
DESDEMONA Well, my good lord.
OTHELLO
Give me your hand. This hand is moist, my lady.
DESDEMONA
It yet has felt no age, and known no sorrow.
OTHELLO
This argues fruitfulness and liberal heart.
Hot, hot and moist. This hand of yours requires
A sequester from liberty, fasting and prayer,
Much castigation, exercise devout;
For there's a young and sweating devil here
That commonly rebels. It is a good hand,
A frank one.
DESDEMONA You may, indeed, say so:
For it was that hand that gave away my heart.
OTHELLO
A liberal hand! The hearts of old gave hands;
But our new heraldry is hands, not hearts.
DESDEMONA
I cannot speak of this. Come now, your promise.
OTHELLO
What promise, chuck?
DESDEMONA
I have sent to bid Cassio come speak with you.

OTHELLO
I have a salt and sorry cold offends me:
Lend me your handkerchief.
DESDEMONA Here, my lord.
OTHELLO
That which I gave you.
DESDEMONA I have it not about me.
OTHELLO
Not?
DESDEMONA No, faith, my lord.
OTHELLO That is a fault.
That handkerchief
Did an Egyptian to my mother give:
She was a charmer and could almost read
The thoughts of people. She told her, while she kept it,
It would make her amiable and subdue my father
Entirely to her love. But, if she lost it
Or made a gift of it, my father's eye
Should hold her loathèd, and his spirits should hunt
After new fancies. She, dying, gave it me,
And bid me, when my fate would have me wive,
To give it her. I did so; and take heed of it:
Make it a darling, like your precious eye.
To lose or give it away were such perdition
As nothing else could match.
DESDEMONA Is it possible?
OTHELLO
It is true: there's magic in the web of it.
A sibyl, that had numbered in the world
The sun to course two hundred compasses,
In her prophetic fury sewed the work:
The worms were hallowed that did breed the silk,
And it was dyed in mummy,[1] which the skilful
Conserved of maidens' hearts.

---

[1]A compound made from mummies or dead bodies.

DESDEMONA Indeed! Is it true?

OTHELLO
Most veritable; therefore look to it well.

DESDEMONA
Then would to God that I had never seen it!

OTHELLO
Ha! Wherefore?

DESDEMONA
Why do you speak so startingly and rash?

OTHELLO
Is it lost? Is it gone? Speak: is it out of the way?

DESDEMONA
Heaven bless us!

OTHELLO Say you?

DESDEMONA It is not lost.
But what if it were?

OTHELLO How!

DESDEMONA
I say it is not lost.

OTHELLO Fetch it: let me see it.

DESDEMONA
Why, so I can, sir; but I will not now.
This is a trick to put me from my suit.
Pray you let Cassio be received again.

OTHELLO
Fetch me the handkerchief: my mind misgives.

DESDEMONA
Come, come:
You'll never meet a more sufficient man.

OTHELLO
The handkerchief!

DESDEMONA I pray, talk to me of Cassio.

OTHELLO
The handkerchief!

DESDEMONA A man that all his time
Has founded his good fortunes on your love;
Shared dangers with you—

OTHELLO
The handkerchief!

DESDEMONA In faith you are to blame.

OTHELLO
Zounds! *Exit*

EMILIA
Is not this man jealous?

DESDEMONA I never saw this before.
Sure, there's some wonder in this handkerchief:
I am most unhappy in the loss of it.

EMILIA
'Tis not a year or two shows us a man.
They are all but stomachs, and we all but food;
They eat us hungerly, and when they are full,
They belch us. Look you, Cassio and my husband.

Enter Iago and Cassio

IAGO
There is no other way: it is she must do it.
And lo, the happiness! Go, and importune her.

DESDEMONA
How now, good Cassio! What's the news with you?

CASSIO
Madam, my former suit. I do beseech you
That by your virtuous means I may again
Exist and be a member of his love;
Whom I, with all the office of my heart,
Entirely honour. I would not be delayed.
If my offence is of such mortal kind
That neither service past, nor present sorrow,
Nor purposed merit in futurity,
Can ransom me into his love again,

But to know so must be my benefit.
So shall I clothe me in a forced content,
And shut myself up in some other course
To Fortune's alms.

DESDEMONA Alas, thrice-gentle Cassio!
My advocation is not now in tune:
My lord is not my lord; nor should I know him,
Were he in feature as in humour altered.
So help me every spirit sanctified
As I have spoken for you all my best,
And stood within the blank of his displeasure
For my free speech! You must awhile be patient.
What I can do, I will; and more I will,
Than for myself I dare. Let that suffice you.

IAGO
Is my lord angry?

EMILIA He went hence but now
And certainly in strange unquietness.

IAGO
Can he be angry? I have seen the cannon
When it has blown his ranks into the air,
And like the devil from his very arm
Puffed his own brother—and can he be angry?
Something of moment then. I will go meet him.
There's matter in it indeed if he is angry.

DESDEMONA
I pray you do so. *Exit Iago*
Something, sure, of state,
Either from Venice, or some unhatched plot
Made demonstrable here in Cyprus to him,
Has puddled his clear spirit. And in such cases
Men's natures wrangle with inferior things,
Though great ones are their object. 'Tis even so.
For let our finger ache, and it endues
Our healthful members even to that sense
Of pain. Nay, we must think men are not gods,

Nor of them look for such observant care
As fits the bridal. Bless me indeed, Emilia,
I was—unhandsome warrior as I am—
Arraigning his unkindness with my soul;
But now I find I had suborned the witness
And he is indicted falsely.

EMILIA
Pray heaven it is state matters, as you think,
And no conception nor any jealous fancy
Concerning you.

DESDEMONA
Alas the day, I never gave him cause.

EMILIA
But jealous souls will not be answered so;
They are not ever jealous for the cause,
But jealous because they're jealous. It is a monster
Begotten upon itself, born on itself.

DESDEMONA
Heaven keep that monster from Othello's mind.

EMILIA
Lady, amen!

DESDEMONA
I will go seek him. Cassio, walk here about.
If I do find him fit, I'll move your suit,
And seek to effect it to my uttermost.

CASSIO
I humbly thank your ladyship.
Exeunt Desdemona and Emilia

Enter Bianca

BIANCA
God save you, friend Cassio.

CASSIO What make you from home?
How is it with you, my most fair Bianca?
In faith, sweet love, I was coming to your house.

BIANCA
And I was going to your lodging, Cassio.
What! Keep a week away? Seven days and nights?
Eight score eight hours? And lovers' absent hours
More tedious than the dial eight score times!
O weary reckoning!

CASSIO Pardon me, Bianca.
I have this while with leaden thoughts been pressed:
But I shall in a more continuate time
Strike off this score of absence. Sweet Bianca,
Take me this work out.

BIANCA O Cassio, whence came this?
This is some token from a newer friend.
To the felt absence now I feel a cause.
Is it come to this? Well, well.

CASSIO Go to, woman!
Throw your vile guesses in the devil's teeth
From whence you have them. You are jealous now
That this is from some mistress, some remembrance:
No, by my faith, Bianca.

BIANCA Why, whose is it?

CASSIO
I know not, sweet. I found it in my chamber.
I like the work well. Ere it be demanded—
As like enough it will—I'd have it copied.
Take it and do it, and leave me for this time.

BIANCA
Leave you? Wherefore?

CASSIO
I do attend here on the General,
And think it no addition, nor my wish,
To have him see me womaned.

BIANCA Why, I pray you?

CASSIO
Not that I love you not.

BIANCA But that you do not love me.
I pray you, bring me on the way a little,
And say if I shall see you soon at night.

CASSIO
It is but a little way that I can bring you,
For I attend here: but I'll see you soon.

BIANCA
'Tis very good: I must await the chance. *Exeunt*

Act IV

SCENE I
Before the citadel.

Enter Othello and Iago

IAGO
Will you think so?
OTHELLO Think so, Iago?
IAGO What!
To kiss in private?
OTHELLO An unauthorized kiss.
IAGO
Or to be naked with her friend in bed
An hour or more, not meaning any harm?
OTHELLO
Naked in bed, Iago, and not mean harm?
It is hypocrisy against the devil.
They that mean virtuously and yet do so,
The devil their virtue tempts, and they tempt heaven.
IAGO
So they do nothing, it is a venial slip.
But if I give my wife a handkerchief—
OTHELLO
What then?
IAGO
Why, then, 'tis hers, my lord, and being hers,
She may, I think, bestow it on any man.
OTHELLO
She is protectress of her honour too.
May she give that?

IAGO
Her honour is an essence that is not seen:
They have it very oft that have it not.
But for the handkerchief—

OTHELLO
By heaven, I would most gladly have forgot it!
You said—O, it comes over my memory
As does the raven over the infected house,
Boding to all!—he had my handkerchief.

IAGO
Ay, what of that?

OTHELLO That's not so good now.

IAGO What
If I had said, I had seen him do you wrong,
Or heard him say—as knaves are such abroad,
Who having by their own importunate suit
Or voluntary dotage of some mistress
Convincèd or supplied them, cannot choose
But they must blab—

OTHELLO Has he said anything?

IAGO
He has, my lord; but be you well assured,
No more than he'll unswear.

OTHELLO What has he said?

IAGO
Faith, that he did—I know not what he did.

OTHELLO
What? What?

IAGO
Lie—

OTHELLO With her?

IAGO With her, on her, what you will.

OTHELLO Lie with her? Lie on her? We say lie on her when they belie her. Lie with her! Zounds, that's fulsome! Handkerchief—confession—handkerchief! To confess and be hanged for his labour. First to be hanged and then to confess! I tremble at it. Nature would not invest herself in such shadowing passion without some instruction. It is not words that shake me thus! Pish! Noses, ears, and lips! Is it possible?—Confess? Handkerchief! O devil!

He falls

IAGO

Work on,
My medicine, work! Thus credulous fools are caught,
And many worthy and chaste dames even thus,
All guiltless, meet reproach. What ho, my lord!
My lord, I say! Othello!

Enter Cassio

How now, Cassio!

CASSIO

What's the matter?

IAGO

My lord is fallen into an epilepsy.
This is his second fit: he had one yesterday.

CASSIO

Rub him about the temples.

IAGO No, forbear.
Unconsciousness must have its quiet course.
If not, he foams at mouth; and by and by
Breaks out to savage madness. Look, he stirs.
Do you withdraw yourself a little while:
He will recover straight. When he is gone,
I would on great occasion speak with you.

Exit Cassio

How is it, General? Have you not hurt your head?

OTHELLO

Do you mock me?

IAGO I mock you? No, by heaven!
Would you would bear your fortune like a man!

OTHELLO
A hornèd man's a monster and a beast.

IAGO
There's many a beast then in a populous city,
And many a civil monster.

OTHELLO
Did he confess it?

IAGO Good sir, be a man.
Think every bearded fellow that's but yoked
May draw with you. There's millions now alive
That nightly lie in those improper beds
Which they dare swear peculiar. Your case is better.
O, it is the spite of hell, the fiend's arch-mock,
To lip a wanton in a secure couch,
And to suppose her chaste! No, let me know;
And knowing what I am, I know what shall be.

OTHELLO
O, you are wise, 'tis certain.

IAGO Stand you awhile apart;
Confine yourself but in a patient mood.
While you were here, overwhelmèd with your grief—
A passion most unsuiting such a man—
Cassio came hither. I shifted him away
And laid a good excuse upon your fit;
Bade him later return and here speak with me,
And this he promised. Do but enclose yourself,
And mark the sneers, the gibes, and notable scorns
That dwell in every region of his face.
For I will make him tell the tale anew,
Where, how, how oft, how long ago, and when
He has, and is again, to meet your wife.
I say, but mark his gestures. For sure, patience!
Or I shall say you're all in all in passion
And nothing of a man.

OTHELLO Do you hear, Iago?
I will be found most cunning in my patience,
But—do you hear?—most bloody.

IAGO That's not amiss,
But yet keep time in all. Will you withdraw?
Othello retires

Now will I question Cassio of Bianca,
A housewife, that by selling her desires
Buys herself bread and clothes. It is a creature
That dotes on Cassio—as 'tis the strumpet's plague
To beguile many and bc beguiled by one.
He, when he hears of her, cannot refrain
From the excess of laughter. Here he comes.

Enter Cassio

As he shall smile, Othello shall go mad;
And his unbookish jealousy must construe
Poor Cassio's smiles, gestures, and light behavior
Quite in the wrong. How do you now, Lieutenant?

CASSIO
The worse in that you give me the addition
Whose want even kills me.

IAGO
Ply Desdemona well and you are sure of it.
Now if this suit lay in Bianca's power,
How quickly should you speed!

CASSIO Alas, poor wretch!

OTHELLO
(*aside*) Look, how he laughs already!

IAGO
I never knew a woman love man so.

CASSIO
Alas, poor rogue! I think in faith she loves me.

OTHELLO
(*aside*) Now he denies it faintly, and laughs it out.

IAGO
Do you hear, Cassio?

OTHELLO
(*aside*) Now he importunes him to tell it over.
Go to, well said, well said!

IAGO
She gives it out that you shall marry her.
Do you intend it?

CASSIO
Ha, ha, ha!

OTHELLO
(*aside*) Do you triumph, Roman? Do you triumph?

CASSIO I marry her! What! A customer! Pray bear some charity to my wit: do not think it so unwholesome. Ha, ha, ha!

OTHELLO (*aside*) So, so, so, so: they laugh that win.

IAGO Faith, the cry goes that you shall marry her.

CASSIO Pray, say true.

IAGO I am a very villain else.

OTHELLO (*aside*) Have you scarred me? Well.

CASSIO This is the monkey's own giving out. She is persuaded I will marry her out of her own love and flattery, not out of my promise.

OTHELLO (*aside*) Iago beckons me. Now he begins the story.

CASSIO She was here even now. She haunts me in every place. I was the other day talking on the sea-bank with certain Venetians, and thither comes the bauble and, by this hand, falls thus about my neck.

OTHELLO (*aside*) Crying 'O dear Cassio!' as it were. His gesture imports it.

CASSIO So hangs and lolls and weeps upon me, so hales and pulls me. Ha, ha, ha!

OTHELLO (*aside*) Now he tells how she plucked him to my chamber. O, I see that nose of yours, but not that dog I shall throw it to!

CASSIO Well, I must leave her company.

IAGO Before me! Look where she comes.

CASSIO 'Tis such another strumpet! Sure, a perfumed one!

Enter Bianca

What do you mean by this haunting of me?

BIANCA Let the devil and his dam haunt you! What did you mean by that same handkerchief you gave me even now? I was a fine fool to take it. I must take out the work! A likely piccc of work, that you should find it in your chamber, and not know who left it there! This is some minx's token, and I must take out the work? There, give it your hobby-horse, wheresoever you had it. I'll take out no work on it.

CASSIO How now, my sweet Bianca! How now, how now!

OTHELLO (*aside*) By heaven, that should be my handkerchief!

BIANCA If you'll come to supper tonight, you may. If you will not, come when you are next prepared for. *Exit*

IAGO After her, after her!

CASSIO Faith I must: she'll rail in the street else.

IAGO Will you sup there?

CASSIO Faith, I intend to.

IAGO Well, I may chance to see you: for I would very gladly speak with you.

CASSIO Pray come, will you?

IAGO Go to! Say no more. *Exit Cassio*

OTHELLO (*coming forward*) How shall I murder him, Iago?

IAGO Did you perceive how he laughed at his vice?

OTHELLO O, Iago!

IAGO And did you see the handkerchief?

OTHELLO Was that mine?

IAGO Yours, by this hand! And to see how he prizes the foolish woman your wife: she gave it him, and he has given it his whore.

OTHELLO I would have him nine years a-killing!—A fine woman, a fair woman, a sweet woman!

IAGO Nay, you must forget that.

OTHELLO Ay, let her rot and perish, and be damned tonight, for she shall not live! No, my heart is turned to stone: I strike it, and it hurts my hand.—O, the world has not a sweeter creature! She might lie by an emperor's side and command him tasks.

IAGO Nay, that's not your way.

OTHELLO Hang her! I do but say what she is: so delicate with her needle, an admirable musician! O, she will sing the savageness out of a bear! Of so high and plenteous wit and invention!

IAGO She is the worse for all this.

OTHELLO O, a thousand, thousand times!—And then of so gentle a condition.

IAGO Ay, too gentle.

OTHELLO Nay, that's certain—but yet the pity of it, Iago! O, Iago, the pity of it, Iago!

IAGO If you are so silly over her iniquity, give her patent to offend, for if it touches not you, it comes near nobody.

OTHELLO I will chop her into bits of meat! Cuckold me!

IAGO O, it is foul in her!

OTHELLO With my officer!

IAGO That is fouler.

OTHELLO Get me some poison, Iago, this night. I'll not expostulate with her, lest her body and beauty unprovide my mind again—this night, Iago.

IAGO Do it not with poison; strangle her in her bed, even the bed she has contaminated.

OTHELLO Good, good! The justice of it pleases; very good!

IAGO And for Cassio, let me be his undertaker. You shall hear more by midnight.

OTHELLO

Excellent good!

Trumpet sounds

What trumpet is that same?

IAGO

I warrant, something from Venice.

Enter Lodovico, Desdemona, and attendants

It is Lodovico,

Come from the Duke; and see your wife is with him.

LODOVICO

God save you, worthy General!

OTHELLO

With all my heart, sir.

LODOVICO

The Duke and Senators of Venice greet you.

He gives him a letter

OTHELLO

I kiss the instrument of their pleasures.

He reads the letter

DESDEMONA

And what's the news, good cousin Lodovico?

IAGO

I am very glad to see you, signior:
Welcome to Cyprus.

LODOVICO

I thank you. How does Lieutenant Cassio?

IAGO

Lives, sir.

DESDEMONA

Cousin, there's fallen between him and my lord
An unkind breach; but you shall make all well.

OTHELLO
Are you sure of that?
DESDEMONA
My lord?
OTHELLO
'This fail you not to do, as you will'—
LODOVICO
He did not call: he's busy in the paper.
Is there division between my lord and Cassio?
DESDEMONA
A most unhappy one; I would do much
To atone them, for the love I bear to Cassio.
OTHELLO
Fire and brimstone!
DESDEMONA
My lord?
OTHELLO
Are you wise?
DESDEMONA
What, is he angry?
LODOVICO Maybe the letter moved him.
For, as I think, they do command him home,
Deputing Cassio in his government.
DESDEMONA
By my faith, I am glad of it.
OTHELLO Indeed!
DESDEMONA My lord?
OTHELLO
I am glad to see you mad.
DESDEMONA Why, sweet Othello!
OTHELLO
Devil!

He strikes her

DESDEMONA
I have not deserved this.
LODOVICO
My lord, this would not be believed in Venice,
Though I should swear I saw it. 'Tis very much.
Make her amends; she weeps.
OTHELLO O devil, devil!
If the earth could conceive with woman's tears,
Each drop she falls would prove a crocodile.
Out of my sight!
DESDEMONA I will not stay to offend you.
LODOVICO
Truly an obedient lady.
I do beseech your lordship call her back.
OTHELLO
Mistress!
DESDEMONA
My lord?
OTHELLO
What would you with her, sir?
LODOVICO
Who? I, my lord?
OTHELLO
Ay, you did wish that I would make her turn.
Sir, she can turn, and turn, and yet go on,
And turn again. And she can weep, sir, weep.
And she's obedient; as you say, obedient,
Very obedient—proceed you in your tears—
Concerning this, sir—O, well-painted passion!—
I am commanded home—get you away!
I'll send for you anon.—Sir, I obey the mandate,
And will return to Venice.—Hence, be gone!
Exit Desdemona

Cassio shall have my place. And sir, tonight
I do entreat that we may sup together.
You are welcome, sir, to Cyprus. Goats and monkeys!
Exit

LODOVICO
Is this the noble Moor, whom our full senate
Call all-in-all sufficient? Is this the nature
Whom passion could not shake? Whose solid virtue
The shot of accident nor dart of chance
Could neither graze nor pierce?

IAGO He is much changed.

LODOVICO
Are his wits safe? Is he not light of brain?

IAGO
He is that he is: I may not breathe my thought
What he might be. If what he might he is not,
I would to heaven he were.

LODOVICO What! Strike his wife!

IAGO
Faith, that was not so well: yet would I knew
That stroke would prove the worst!

LODOVICO Is it his use?
Or did the letters work upon his blood
And new-create this fault?

IAGO Alas, alas!
It is not honesty in me to speak
What I have seen and known. You shall observe him,
And his own courses will denote him so,
That I may save my speech. Do but go after,
And mark how he continues.

LODOVICO
I am sorry that I am deceived in him.

SCENE II
The citadel.

Enter Othello and Emilia

OTHELLO
You have seen nothing then?

EMILIA
Nor ever heard, nor ever did suspect.

OTHELLO
Yes, you have seen Cassio and her together.

EMILIA
But then I saw no harm; and then I heard
Each syllable that breath made up between them.

OTHELLO
What! Did they never whisper?

EMILIA Never, my lord.

OTHELLO
Nor send you out of the way?

EMILIA Never.

OTHELLO
To fetch her fan, her gloves, her mask, nor anything?

EMILIA
Never, my lord.

OTHELLO
That is strange.

EMILIA
I durst, my lord, to wager she is chaste,
Lay down my soul at stake. If you think otherwise
Remove your thought: it does abuse your bosom.
If any wretch has put this in your head,
Let heaven requite it with the serpent's curse!
For if she is not honest, chaste, and true,
There's no man happy. The purest of their wives
Is foul as slander.

OTHELLO Bid her come hither: go!

Exit Emilia

She says enough; yet she's a simple bawd
That cannot say as much. This is a subtle whore,
A closet lock and key of villainous secrets;
And yet she'll kneel and pray—I have seen her do it.

Enter Desdemona and Emilia

DESDEMONA
My lord, what is your will?

OTHELLO Pray, chuck, come hither.

DESDEMONA
What is your pleasure?

OTHELLO Let me see your eyes.
Look in my face.

DESDEMONA What horrible fancy is this?

OTHELLO (*to Emilia*)
Some of your function, mistress.
Leave procreants alone and shut the door.
Cough or cry 'hem' if anybody comes.
Your mystery, your mystery! Nay, dispatch! *Exit Emilia*

DESDEMONA
Upon my knees, what does your speech import?
I understand a fury in your words,
But not the words.

OTHELLO Why, what are you?

DESDEMONA
Your wife, my lord; your true and loyal wife.

OTHELLO
Come, swear it; damn yourself;
Lest being like one of heaven, the devils themselves
Should fear to seize you. Therefore be double-damned:
Swear you are chaste.

DESDEMONA Heaven does truly know it.

OTHELLO
Heaven truly knows that you are false as hell.
DESDEMONA
To whom, my lord? With whom? How am I false?
OTHELLO
Ah, Desdèmon! Away, away, away!
DESDEMONA
Alas, the heavy day! Why do you weep?
Am I the motive of these tears my lord?
If haply you my father do suspect
An instrument of this your calling back,
Lay not your blame on me. If you have lost him,
I have lost him too.
OTHELLO Had it pleased heaven
To try me with affliction, had they rained
All kind of sores and shames on my bare head,
Steeped me in poverty to the very lips,
Given to captivity me and my utmost hopes,
I should have found in some place of my soul
A drop of patience. But alas, to make me
A fixèd figure for the time of scorn
To point its slow unmoving finger at!
Yet could I bear that too, well, very well:
But there where I have garnered up my heart,
Where either I must live, or bear no life,
The fountain now from which my current runs,
Or else dries up—to be discarded thence
Or keep it as a cistern for foul toads
To knot and gender in! Turn your complexion there,
Patience, you young and rose-lipped cherubin,
Ay, there look grim as hell!
DESDEMONA
I hope my noble lord esteems me chaste.
OTHELLO
O, ay! As summer flies are in the shambles,
That quicken even with blowing, O, you weed,

Who are so lovely fair, and smell so sweet
That the sense aches at you, would you had never been
born!

DESDEMONA
Alas, what ignorant sin have I committed?

OTHELLO
Was this fair paper, this most goodly book,
Made to write 'whore' upon? What committed!
Committed? O, you public commoner!
I should make very forges of my cheeks,
That would to cinders burn up modesty,
Did I but speak your deeds. What committed?
Heaven stops the nose at it, and the moon winks;
The bawdy wind, that kisses all it meets,
Is hushed within the hollow mine of earth
And will not hear it. What committed?
Impudent strumpet!

DESDEMONA By heaven, you do me wrong.

OTHELLO
Are you not a strumpet?

DESDEMONA No, as I am a Christian.
If to preserve this vessel for my lord
From any other foul unlawful touch,
Be not to be a strumpet, I am none.

OTHELLO
What! Not a whore?

DESDEMONA No, as I shall be saved.

OTHELLO
Is it possible?

DESDEMONA
O, heaven forgive us!

OTHELLO I cry you mercy then:
I took you for that cunning whore of Venice
That married with Othello. (*Calling*) You, mistress,
That have the office opposite to Saint Peter
And keep the gate of hell!

Enter Emilia

You, you, ay, you!
We have done our course: there's money for your pains.
I pray you turn the key, and keep our counsel. *Exit*

EMILIA
Alas, what does this gentleman conceive?
How do you, madam? How do you, my good lady?

DESDEMONA
Faith, half asleep.

EMILIA
Good madam, what's the matter with my lord?

DESDEMONA
With whom?

EMILIA
Why, with my lord, madam.

DESDEMONA
Who is your lord?

EMILIA He that is yours, sweet lady.

DESDEMONA
I have none. Do not talk to me, Emilia:
I cannot weep; and answers have I none,
But what should go by water. Pray you tonight
Lay on my bed my wedding sheets, remember,
And call your husband hither

EMILIA Here's a change indeed!
Exit

DESDEMONA
It is meet I should be used so, very meet.
How have I behaved, that he might stick
The smallest opinion on my least misuse?

Enter Emilia and Iago

IAGO
What is your pleasure, madam? How is it with you?

DESDEMONA
I cannot tell: those that do teach young babes
Do it with gentle means and easy tasks:
He might have chidden me so, for, in good faith,
I am a child to chiding.

IAGO
What is the matter, lady?

EMILIA
Alas, Iago, my lord has so bewhored her,
Thrown such despite and heavy terms upon her
As true heart cannot bear.

DESDEMONA
Am I that name, Iago?

IAGO
What name, fair lady?

DESDEMONA
Such as she said my lord did say I was.

EMILIA
He called her whore: a beggar in his drink
Could not have laid such terms upon his strumpet.

IAGO
Why did he so?

DESDEMONA
I do not know: I am sure I am none such.

IAGO
Do not weep, do not weep. Alas the day!

EMILIA
Did she forsake so many noble matches,
Her father, and her country, all her friends,
To be called whore? Would it not make one weep?

DESDEMONA
It is my wretched fortune.

IAGO
Curse him for it!
How comes this whim upon him?

DESDEMONA
Nay, heaven does know.

EMILIA
I will be hanged if some eternal villain,
Some busy and insinuating rogue,

Some lying, cozening slave, to get some office,
Has not devised this slander; I'll be hanged else.

IAGO

Fie, there is no such man! It is impossible.

DESDEMONA

If any such there is, heaven pardon him.

EMILIA

A halter pardon him and hell gnaw his bones!
Why should he call her whore? Who keeps her company?
What place, what time, what form, what likelihood?
The Moor's abused by some most villainous knave,
Some base notorious knave, some scurvy fellow.
O heaven, that such companions you'd unfold,
And put in every honest hand a whip
To lash the rascals naked through the world,
Even from the east to the west!

IAGO Speak within door.

EMILIA

O fie upon them! Some such squire he was
That turned your wit the seamy side without
And made you to suspect me with the Moor.

IAGO

You are a fool, go to.

DESDEMONA O good Iago,
What shall I do to win my lord again?
Good friend, go to him; for, by this light of heaven,
I know not how I lost him. Here I kneel:
If ever my will did trespass against his love,
Either in discourse of thought or actual deed;
Or that my eyes, my ears, or any sense
Delighted them in any other form;
Or that I do not yet, and ever did,
And ever will—though he does shake me off
To beggarly divorcement—love him dearly,
Comfort forswear me! Unkindness may do much,
And his unkindness may defeat my life,

But never taint my love. I cannot say 'whore':
It does abhor me now I speak the word;
To do the act that might the addition earn
Not the world's mass of vanity could make me.

IAGO
I pray you, be content: 'tis but his humour;
The business of the state does him offence,
And he does chide with you.

DESDEMONA
If it were no other—

IAGO It is so, I warrant.
Hark how these instruments summon to supper!
The messengers of Venice stay the meat.
Go in, and weep not; all things shall be well.
Exeunt Desdemona and Emilia

Enter Roderigo

How now, Roderigo?

RODERIGO I do not find that you deal justly with me.

IAGO What in the contrary?

RODERIGO Every day you put me off with some device, Iago, and rather, as it seems to me now, keep from me all conveniency, than supply me with the least advantage of hope. I will indeed no longer endure it. Nor am I yet persuaded to put up in peace what already I have foolishly suffered.

IAGO Will you hear me, Roderigo?

RODERIGO Faith, I have heard too much; for your words and performances are no kin together.

IAGO You charge me most unjustly.

RODERIGO With naught but truth. I have wasted myself out of my means. The jewels you have had from me to deliver to Desdemona would half have corrupted a votarist. You have told me she has received them, and returned me expectations and comforts of sudden respect and acquaintance, but I find none.

IAGO Well, go to; very well.

RODERIGO Very well, go to! I cannot go to, man, and it is not very well. Nay, I think it is scurvy and begin to find myself cheated in it.

IAGO Very well.

RODERIGO I tell you, it is not very well. I will make myself known to Desdemona. If she will return me my jewels, I will give over my suit and repent my unlawful solicitation. If not, assure yourself I will seek satisfaction of you.

IAGO You have said now.

RODERIGO Ay, and said nothing but what I protest intention of doing.

IAGO Why, now I see there's mettle in you; and even from this instant do build on you a better opinion than ever before. Give me your hand, Roderigo. You have taken against me a most just exception; but yet I protest I have dealt most directly in your affair.

RODERIGO It has not appeared.

IAGO I grant indeed it has not appeared; and your suspicion is not without wit and judgement. But, Roderigo, if you have that in you indeed, which I have greater reason to believe now than ever—I mean purpose, courage, and valour—this night show it. If you the next night following enjoy not Desdemona, take me from this world with treachery, and devise engines for my life.

RODERIGO Well, what is it? Is it within reason and compass?

IAGO Sir, there is especial commission come from Venice to depute Cassio in Othello's place.

RODERIGO Is that true? Why, then Othello and Desdemona return again to Venice.

IAGO O, no: he goes into Mauritania and takes away with him the fair Desdemona, unless his abode be lingered here by some accident: wherein none can be so determinate as the removing of Cassio.

RODERIGO How do you mean 'removing' of him?

IAGO Why, by making him incapable of Othello's place—knocking out his brains.

RODERIGO And that you would have me to do?

IAGO Ay, if you dare do yourself a profit and a right. He sups tonight with a harlot; and thither will I go to him. He knows not yet of his honourable fortune. If you will watch his going thence—which I will fashion to fall out between twelve and one—you may take him at your pleasure. I will be near to second your attempt, and he shall fall between us. Come, stand not amazed at it, but go along with me. I will show you such a necessity in his death that you shall think yourself bound to put it on him. It is now high supper-time and the night grows to waste. About it!

RODERIGO I will hear further reason for this.

IAGO And you shall be satisfied. *Exeunt*

SCENE III
The same.

Enter Othello, Lodovico, Desdemona, Emilia, and attendants

LODOVICO
I do beseech you, sir, trouble yourself no further.

OTHELLO
O, pardon me: it will do me good to walk.

LODOVICO
Madam, good night. I humbly thank your ladyship.

DESDEMONA
Your honour is most welcome.

OTHELLO Will you walk, sir?
O, Desdemona!
DESDEMONA
My lord?
OTHELLO Get you to bed on the instant. I will return forthwith. Dismiss your attendant there. Look it be done.
DESDEMONA I will, my lord.
Exeunt Othello, Lodovico, and attendants
EMILIA
How goes it now? He looks gentler than he did.
DESDEMONA
He says he will return incontinent.
He has commanded me to go to bed,
And bade me to dismiss you.
EMILIA Dismiss me?
DESDEMONA
It was his bidding: therefore, good Emilia,
Give me my nightly wearing, and adieu.
We must not now displease him.
EMILIA
I would you had never seen him.
DESDEMONA
So would not I: my love does so approve him
That even his stubbornness, his checks, his frowns—
Pray, unpin me—have grace and favour in them.
EMILIA
I have laid those sheets, you bade me, on the bed.
DESDEMONA
All's one. Good faith, how foolish are our minds!
If I do die before you, pray shroud me
In one of those same sheets.
EMILIA Come, come, you talk.
DESDEMONA
My mother had a maid called Barbary:
She was in love: and him she loved proved mad

And did forsake her. She had a song of willow;
An old thing it was; but it expressed her fortune,
And she died singing it. That song tonight
Will not go from my mind: I have much to do
But to go hang my head all at one side,
And sing it like poor Barbary—pray, be quick.

EMILIA
Shall I go fetch your night-gown?

DESDEMONA
No, unpin me here.
This Lodovico is a proper man.

EMILIA
A very handsome man.

DESDEMONA
He speaks well.

EMILIA I know a lady in Venice would have walked barefoot to Palestine for a touch of his nether lip.

DESDEMONA (*sings*)
The poor soul sat sighing by a sycamore tree,
Sing all a green willow;
Her hand on her bosom, her head on her knee,
Sing willow, willow, willow;
The fresh streams ran by her and murmured her moans;
Sing willow, willow, willow;
Her salt tears fell from her and softened the stones—
Lay by these.
Sing willow, willow, willow—
Pray make haste; he'll come anon.
Sing all a green willow must be my garland.
Let nobody blame him; his scorn I approve—
Nay, that's not next. Hark, who is it that knocks?

EMILIA It's the wind.

DESDEMONA
I called my love false love, but what said he then?
Sing willow, willow, willow:
If I court more women, you'll couch with more men.

So get you gone; good night. My eyes do itch:
Does that bode weeping?

EMILIA 'Tis neither here nor there.

DESDEMONA
I have heard it said so. O, these men, these men!
Do you in conscience think—tell me, Emilia—
That there are women who abuse their husbands
In such gross kind?

EMILIA There are some such, no question.

DESDEMONA
Would you do such a deed for all the world?

EMILIA
Why, would not you?

DESDEMONA No, by this heavenly light.

EMILIA Nor I neither by this heavenly light: I might do it as well in the dark.

DESDEMONA Would you do such a deed for all the world?

EMILIA The world's a huge thing: it is a great price for a small vice.

DESDEMONA In truth, I think you would not.

EMILIA In truth I think I should, and undo it when I had done it. Sure, I would not do such a thing for a joint ring, nor for measures of lawn, nor for gowns, petticoats, nor caps, nor any petty exhibition. But for all the whole world! God's pity, who would not make her husband a cuckold, to make him a monarch? I should venture purgatory for it.

DESDEMONA Bless me, if I would do such a wrong for the whole world!

EMILIA Why, the wrong is but a wrong in the world; and having the world for your labour, 'tis a wrong in your own world, and you might quickly make it right.

DESDEMONA I do not think there is any such woman.

EMILIA Yes, a dozen: and as many in addition as would store the world they played for.
But I do think it is their husbands' faults

If wives do fall. Say that they slack their duties,
And pour our treasures into foreign laps;
Or else break out in peevish jealousies,
Throwing restraint upon us; or say they strike us,
Or scant our former living out of spite—
Why, we have galls, and though we have some grace,
Yet have we some revenge. Let husbands know
Their wives have sense like them: they see and smell,
And have their palates both for sweet and sour
As husbands have. What is it that they do,
When they change us for others? Is it sport?
I think it is. And does affection breed it?
I think it does. Is it frailty that thus errs?
It is so too. And have not we affections,
Desires for sport, and frailty, as men have?
Then let them use us well: else let them know
The ills we do, their ills instruct us so.

DESDEMONA

Good night, good night. God me such uses send,
Not to pick bad from bad, but by bad mend! *Exeunt*

Act V

SCENE I
A street.

Enter Iago and Roderigo

IAGO
Here, stand behind this bulk: straight will he come.
Wear your good rapier bare, and put it home.
Quick, quick; fear nothing: I'll be at your elbow.
It makes us, or it mars us; think on that,
And fix most firm your resolution.

RODERIGO
Be near at hand; I may miscarry in it.

IAGO
Here, at your hand: be bold, and take your stand.
He retires

RODERIGO
I have no great devotion to the deed,
And yet he has given me satisfying reasons.
'Tis but a man gone. Forth my sword! He dies!

IAGO
I have rubbed this young scab almost to the quick,
And he grows angry. Now, whether he kills Cassio,
Or Cassio him, or each does kill the other,
Every way makes my gain. Live Roderigo,
He calls me to a restitution large
Of gold and jewels, that I swindled from him
As gifts to Desdemona.
It must not be. If Cassio does remain
He has a daily beauty in his life

That makes me ugly: and besides, the Moor
May reveal me to him—there stand I in much peril.
No, he must die. But soft, I hear him coming.

Enter Cassio

RODERIGO
I know his gait; 'tis he. Villain, you die!

CASSIO
That thrust had been my enemy indeed,
But that my coat is better than you think.
I will make proof of yours.

He wounds Roderigo

RODERIGO O, I am slain!

Iago wounds Cassio in the leg, and exit

CASSIO
I am maimed for ever. Help, ho! Murder, murder!

Enter Othello, above

OTHELLO
The voice of Cassio: Iago keeps his word.

RODERIGO
O, villain that I am!

OTHELLO It is even so.

CASSIO
O, help, ho! Light! A surgeon!

OTHELLO
'Tis he! O brave Iago, honest and just,
That have such noble sense of your friend's wrong,
You teach me! Minion, your dear lies dead,
And your unblest fate hastes. Strumpet, I come!
Forth of my heart those charms, your eyes, are blotted;
Your bed, lust-stained, shall with lust's blood be spotted.

Exit Othello

Enter Lodovico and Gratiano

CASSIO
What, ho! No watch? No passage? Murder, murder!

GRATIANO
'Tis some mischance: the cry is very direful.

CASSIO
O, help!

LODOVICO
Hark!

RODERIGO
O wretched villain!

LODOVICO
Two or three groan. It is a heavy night.
These may be counterfeits. Let's think it unsafe
To come in to the cry without more help.

RODERIGO
Nobody come? Then shall I bleed to death.

LODOVICO
Hark!

Enter Iago, with a light

GRATIANO
Here's one comes in his shirt, with light and weapons.

IAGO
Who's there? Whose noise is this that cries on murder?

LODOVICO
We do not know.

IAGO Did you not hear a cry?

CASSIO
Here, here: for heaven's sake help me!

IAGO What's the matter?

GRATIANO
This is Othello's Ensign, as I take it.
LODOVICO
The same indeed, a very valiant fellow.
IAGO
What are you here, that cry so grievously?
CASSIO
Iago? O, I am spoiled, undone by villains!
Give me some help.
IAGO
O me, Lieutenant! What villains have done this?
CASSIO
I think that one of them is hereabout
And cannot make away.
IAGO O treacherous villains!
What are you there? Come in, and give some help.
RODERIGO
O, help me here!
CASSIO
That's one of them.
IAGO O murderous slave! O villain!

He stabs Roderigo

RODERIGO
O damned Iago! O inhuman dog!
IAGO
Kill men in the dark? Where are these bloody thieves?
How silent is this town! Ho, murder, murder!

Lodovico and Gratiano come forward

What may you be? Are you of good or evil?
LODOVICO
As you shall prove us, praise us.

IAGO
Signior Lodovico?

LODOVICO
He, sir.

IAGO
I cry you mercy. Here's Cassio hurt by villains.

GRATIANO
Cassio?

IAGO
How is it, brother?

CASSIO
My leg is cut in two.

IAGO God, heaven forbid!
Light, gentlemen. I'll bind it with my shirt.

Enter Bianca

BIANCA
What is the matter, ho? Who is it that cried?

IAGO
Who is it that cried?

BIANCA
O, my dear Cassio, my sweet Cassio,
O Cassio, Cassio, Cassio!

IAGO
O notable strumpet! Cassio, may you suspect
Who they should be that have thus mangled you?

CASSIO
No.

GRATIANO
I am sorry to find you thus: I have been to seek you.

IAGO
Lend me a garter: so. O, for a chair
To bear him easily hence!

BIANCA Alas, he faints!
O Cassio, Cassio, Cassio!

IAGO

Gentlemen all, I do suspect this trash
To be a party in this injury.
Patience awhile, good Cassio. Come, come,
Lend me a light. Know we this face or no?
Alas, my friend, and my dear countryman
Roderigo? No—yes, sure—O heaven, Roderigo!

GRATIANO

What! Of Venice?

IAGO

Even he, sir. Did you know him?

GRATIANO Know him? Ay.

IAGO

Signor Gratiano? I cry you gentle pardon.
These bloody accidents must excuse my manners
That so neglected you.

GRATIANO I am glad to see you.

IAGO

How do you, Cassio? O, a chair, a chair!

GRATIANO

Roderigo!

IAGO

He, he, 'tis he.

Enter attendants with chair

O, that's well said, the chair!
Some good man bear him carefully from hence.
I'll fetch the General's surgeon. For you, mistress,
Save you your labour. He that lies slain here, Cassio,
Was my dear friend. What malice was between you?

CASSIO

None in the world, nor do I know the man.

IAGO

(*to Bianca*) What, look you pale? O, bear him out of the air.

Cassio and Roderigo are borne off

Stay you, good gentlemen. Look you pale, mistress?
Do you perceive the wildness of her eye?
Nay, if you stare, we shall hear more anon.
Behold her well; I pray you look upon her.
Do you see, gentlemen? Nay, guiltiness will speak
Though tongues were out of use.

Enter Emilia

EMILIA

Alas, what's the matter? What's the matter, husband?

IAGO

Cassio has here been set on in the dark
By Roderigo and fellows that are escaped:
He's almost slain and Roderigo quite.

EMILIA

Alas, good gentleman! Alas, good Cassio!

IAGO

This is the fruit of whoring. Pray, Emilia,
Go know of Cassio where he supped tonight.
What, do you shake at that?

BIANCA

He supped at my house, but I therefore shake not.

IAGO

O, did he so? I charge you go with me.

EMILIA

O, fie upon you, strumpet!

BIANCA

I am no strumpet, but of life as honest
As you that thus abuse me.

EMILIA As I? Foh! Fie upon you!

IAGO

Kind gentlemen, let's see poor Cassio dressed.
Come, mistress, you must tell us another tale.
Emilia, run you to the citadel,
And tell my lord and lady what has happened.
Will you go on before? (*Aside*) This is the night
That either makes me, or undoes me quite. *Exeunt*

SCENE II
The citadel. A bedchamber.

Enter Othello, with a light, Desdemona in her bed

OTHELLO

It is the cause, it is the cause, my soul:
Let me not name it to you, you chaste stars!
It is the cause. Yet I'll not shed her blood,
Nor scar that whiter skin of hers than snow,
And smooth as monumental alabaster.
Yet she must die, else she'll betray more men.
Put out the light, and then put out the light:
If I quench you, you flaming minister,
I can again your former light restore,
Should I repent me. But once put out your light,
You cunningest pattern of excelling nature,
I know not where is that Promethean heat
That can your light relume. When I have plucked your rose,
I cannot give it vital growth again,
It needs must wither. I'll smell it on the tree.

He kisses her

O balmy breath, that do almost persuade
Justice to break its sword! One more, one more.

Be thus when you are dead and I will kill you,
And love you after. One more, and this the last.
So sweet was never so fatal. I must weep.
But they are cruel tears: this sorrow's heavenly—
It strikes where it does love. She wakes.

DESDEMONA
Who's there? Othello?

OTHELLO
Ay, Desdemona.

DESDEMONA Will you come to bed, my lord?

OTHELLO
Have you prayed tonight, Desdemon?

DESDEMONA Ay, my lord.

OTHELLO
If you bethink yourself of any crime
Unreconciled as yet to heaven and grace,
Solicit for it straight.

DESDEMONA
Alas, my lord, what may you mean by that?

OTHELLO
Well, do it, and be brief; I will walk by:
I would not kill your unpreparèd spirit;
No—heaven forfend!—I would not kill your soul.

DESDEMONA
Talk you of killing?

OTHELLO Ay, I do.

DESDEMONA Then heaven
Have mercy on me!

OTHELLO Amen, with all my heart!

DESDEMONA
If you say so, I hope you will not kill me.

OTHELLO
Hum!

DESDEMONA
And yet I fear you: for you are fatal then
When your eyes roll so. Why I should fear I know not,
Since guiltiness I know not; but yet I feel I fear.

OTHELLO
Think on your sins.

DESDEMONA They are loves I bear to you.

OTHELLO
Ay, and for that you die.

DESDEMONA
That death's unnatural that kills for loving.
Alas, why gnaw you so your nether lip?
Some bloody passion shakes your very frame:
These are portents; but yet I hope, I hope
They do not point on me.

OTHELLO Peace, and be still!

DESDEMONA
I will—so. What is the matter?

OTHELLO
That handkerchief which I so loved and gave you,
You gave to Cassio.

DESDEMONA No, by my life and soul!
Send for the man and ask him.

OTHELLO Sweet soul, take heed,
Take heed of perjury: you are on your death-bed.

DESDEMONA
Ay, but not yet to die.

OTHELLO Yes, now at once.
Therefore confess you freely of your sin;
For to deny each article with oath
Cannot remove nor choke the strong conception
That I do groan with. For you are to die.

DESDEMONA
Then Lord have mercy on me!

OTHELLO I say, amen.

DESDEMONA
And have you mercy too! I never did
Offend you in my life; never loved Cassio
But with such general warranty of heaven
As I might love. I never gave him token.

OTHELLO
By heaven, I saw my handkerchief in his hand!
O perjured woman! You do stone my heart,
And make me call what I intend to do
A murder, which I thought a sacrifice.
I saw the handkerchief.

DESDEMONA He found it then.
I never gave it him. Send for him hither.
Let him confess a truth.

OTHELLO He has confessed.

DESDEMONA
What, my lord?

OTHELLO
That he has used you.

DESDEMONA How? Unlawfully?

OTHELLO
Ay.

DESDEMONA
He will not say so.

OTHELLO No, his mouth is stopped:
Honest Iago has taken order for it.

DESDEMONA
O, my fear interprets! What, is he dead?

OTHELLO
Had all his hairs been lives, my great revenge
Had stomach for them all.

DESDEMONA
Alas, he is betrayed, and I undone.

OTHELLO
Out, strumpet! Weep you for him to my face?

DESDEMONA
O banish me, my lord, but kill me not!
OTHELLO
Down, strumpet!
DESDEMONA
Kill me tomorrow: let me live tonight!
OTHELLO
Nay, if you strive—
DESDEMONA
But half an hour!
OTHELLO Being done, there is no pause.
DESDEMONA
But while I say one prayer!
OTHELLO It is too late.
DESDEMONA
O Lord, Lord, Lord!

He smothers her

EMILIA
(*without*) My lord, my lord! What, ho! My lord, my lord!
OTHELLO
What noise is this? Not dead? Not yet quite dead?
I, that am cruel, am yet merciful:
I would not have you linger in your pain.
So, so.
EMILIA (*without*) What, ho! My lord, my lord!
OTHELLO Who's there?
EMILIA
(*without*) O, good my lord, I'd speak a word with you.
OTHELLO
Yes, 'tis Emilia.—By and by.—She's dead.
'Tis like she comes to speak of Cassio's death:
The noise was high. Ha! No more moving?
Still as the grave. Shall she come in? Were it good?

I think she stirs again. No. What's best to do?
If she comes in, she'll sure speak to my wife—
My wife! My wife! What wife? I have no wife.
O, insupportable! O heavy hour!
I think it should be now a huge eclipse
Of sun and moon, and that the affrighted globe
Should yawn at alteration.

EMILIA I do beseech you
That I may speak with you. O, good my lord!

OTHELLO
I had forgotten you. O, come in, Emilia.
Soft; by and by. Let me the curtains draw.
Where are you? (*He unlocks door.*) What's the matter with you now?

Enter Emilia

EMILIA
O, my good lord, yonder's foul murder done.

OTHELLO
What! Now?

EMILIA
But now, my lord.

OTHELLO
It is the very error of the moon;
She comes more near to earth than she was wont,
And makes men mad.

EMILIA
Cassio, my lord, has killed a young Venetian
Called Roderigo

OTHELLO Roderigo killed?
And Cassio killed?

EMILIA No, Cassio is not killed.

OTHELLO
Not Cassio killed! Then murder is out of tune,
And sweet revenge grows harsh.

DESDEMONA
O, falsely, falsely murdered!
EMILIA
O Lord! What cry is that?
OTHELLO
That? What?
EMILIA
Out and alas, that was my lady's voice!

She draws back the curtains

Help, help, ho, help! O, lady, speak again!
Sweet Desdemona, O sweet mistress, speak!
DESDEMONA
A guiltless death I die.
EMILIA
O, who has done this deed?
DESDEMONA
Nobody—I myself—farewell.
Commend me to my kind lord—O, farewell! *She dies*
OTHELLO
Why, how should she be murdered?
EMILIA
Alas, who knows?
OTHELLO
You heard her say herself it was not I.
EMILIA
She said so: I must needs report the truth.
OTHELLO
She's like a liar gone to burning hell:
'Twas I that killed her.
EMILIA
O, the more angel she,
And you the blacker devil!
OTHELLO
She turned to folly; and she was a whore.
EMILIA
You do belie her, and you are a devil.

OTHELLO
She was false as water.

EMILIA You are rash as fire to say
That she was false. O, she was heavenly true!

OTHELLO
Cassio did top her: ask your husband else.
O, I were damned beneath all depth in hell
But that I did proceed upon just grounds
To this extremity. Your husband knew it all.

EMILIA
My husband!

OTHELLO Your husband.

EMILIA That she was false to wedlock?

OTHELLO
Ay, with Cassio. Nay, had she been true,
If heaven would make me such another world
Of one entire and perfect chrysolite,
I'd not have sold her for it.

EMILIA My husband!

OTHELLO
Ay, 'twas he that told me on her first:
An honest man he is, and hates the slime
That sticks on filthy deeds.

EMILIA My husband!

OTHELLO
What needs this iterance, woman? I say your husband.

EMILIA
O mistress, villainy has made mocks with love!
My husband say that she was false?

OTHELLO He, woman;
I say your husband; do you understand the word?
My friend, your husband, honest, honest Iago.

EMILIA
If he says so, may his pernicious soul
Rot half a grain a day! He lies to the heart.
She was too fond of her most filthy bargain.

OTHELLO
Ha!
EMILIA
Do your worst:
This deed of yours is no more worthy heaven
Than you were worthy her.
OTHELLO Peace, you were best.
EMILIA
You have not half that power to do me harm
As I have to be hurt. O gull! O dolt!
As ignorant as dirt! You have done a deed—
I care not for your sword—I'll make you known,
Though I lost twenty lives. Help! Help, ho! Help!
The Moor has killed my mistress! Murder! Murder!

Enter Montano, Gratiano, and Iago

MONTANO
What is the matter? How now, General?
EMILIA
O, are you come, Iago? You have done well,
That men must lay their murders on your neck.
GRATIANO
What is the matter?
EMILIA
Disprove this villain, if you are a man:
He says you told him that his wife was false.
I know you did not: you're not such a villain.
Speak, for my heart is full.
IAGO
I told him what I thought, and told no more
Than what he found himself was apt and true.
EMILIA
But did you ever tell him she was false?
IAGO
I did.

EMILIA
You told a lie, an odious damnèd lie:
Upon my soul, a lie, a wicked lie!
She false with Cassio! Did you say with Cassio?

IAGO
With Cassio, mistress! Shut up, charm your tongue.

EMILIA
I will not charm my tongue; I am bound to speak:
My mistress here lies murdered in her bed.

ALL
O heavens forfend!

EMILIA
And your reports have set the murder on.

OTHELLO
Nay, stare not masters: it is true indeed.

GRATIANO
It is a strange truth.

MONTANO
O monstrous act!

EMILIA Villainy, villainy, villainy!
I think upon it, I think—I smell it—O villainy!
I thought so then; I'll kill myself for grief.
O villainy, villainy!

IAGO
What, are you mad? I charge you get you home.

EMILIA
Good gentlemen, let me have leave to speak.
'Tis proper I obey him, but not now.
Perhaps, Iago, I will never go home.

OTHELLO
(falling on bed) O! O! O!

EMILIA Nay, lay you down and roar,
For you have killed the sweetest innocent
That ever did lift up eye.

OTHELLO *(rising)* O, she was foul!
I scarce did know you, uncle; there lies your niece,

Whose breath indeed these hands have newly stopped.
I know this act shows horrible and grim.

GRATIANO

Poor Desdemon, I am glad your father's dead:
Your match was mortal to him, and pure grief
Cut his old thread in twain. Did he live now,
This sight would make him do a desperate deed,
Yea, curse his better angel from his side,
And fall to damnation.

OTHELLO

'Tis pitiful: but yet Iago knows
That she with Cassio has the act of shame
A thousand times committed. Cassio confessed it,
And she did gratify his amorous works
With that recognizance and pledge of love
Which I first gave her. I saw it in his hand:
It was a handkerchief, an antique token
My father gave my mother.

EMILIA O God! O heavenly Powers!

IAGO

Zounds, hold your peace!

EMILIA 'Twill out, 'twill out. I peace?
No, I will speak as liberal as the north;
Let heaven, and men, and devils, let them all,
All, all cry shame against me, yet I'll speak.

IAGO

Be wise, and get you home.

EMILIA I will not.

Iago draws his sword

GRATIANO Fie!
Your sword upon a woman!

EMILIA

O you dull Moor, that handkerchief you speak of
I found by fortune and did give my husband,

For often, with a solemn earnestness—
More than indeed belonged to such a trifle—
He begged of me to steal it.

IAGO Villainous whore!

EMILIA
She give it Cassio? No, alas, I found it
And I did give it my husband.

IAGO Filth, you lie!

EMILIA
By heaven I do not, I do not, gentlemen.
O murderous coxcomb, what should such a fool
Do with so good a wife?

OTHELLO Are there no stones in heaven
But what serve for the thunder? Precious villain!

He runs at Iago; Montano disarms him; Iago stabs Emilia from behind and exit

GRATIANO
The woman falls: sure he has killed his wife.

EMILIA
Ay, ay: O, lay me by my mistress' side.

GRATIANO
He's gone, but his wife is killed.

MONTANO
'Tis a notorious villain. Take you this weapon,
Which I have here recovered from the Moor.
Come guard the door without: let him not pass,
But kill him rather. I'll after that same villain,
For 'tis a damnèd slave.

Exeunt Montano and Gratiano

OTHELLO I am not valiant either,
But every puny swordsman gets my sword.
But why should honour outlive honesty?
Let it go all.

EMILIA What did your song bode, lady?
Hark, can you hear me? I will play the swan
And die in music. (*Singing*) Willow, willow, willow.
Moor, she was chaste; she loved you, cruel Moor,
So come my soul to bliss, as I speak true;
So speaking as I think, I die, I die. *She dies*

OTHELLO
I have another weapon in this chamber:
It was a sword of Spain, the ice-brook's temper.
O, here it is. Uncle, I must come forth.

GRATIANO
(*within*) If you attempt it, it will cost you dear;
You have no weapon, and perforce must suffer.

OTHELLO
Look in upon me then, and speak with me,
Or naked as I am I will assault you.

Enter Gratiano

GRATIANO
What is the matter?

OTHELLO Behold, I have a weapon:
A better never did itself sustain
Upon a soldier's thigh. I have seen the day
That with this little arm and this good sword,
I have made my way through more impediments
Than twenty times your stop. But, O vain boast!—
Who can control his fate?—It is not so now.
Be not afraid, though you do see me weaponed:
Here is my journey's end, here is my butt
And very sea-mark of my utmost sail.
Do you go back dismayed? It is a lost fear:
Man but a rush against Othello's breast,
And he retires. Where should Othello go?

He goes to the bed

Now, how do you look now? O ill-starred wench!
Pale as your smock! When we shall meet at Doom
This look of yours will hurl my soul from heaven
And fiends will snatch at it. Cold, cold, my girl,
Even like your chastity.
O cursèd, cursèd slave! Whip me, ye devils,
From the possession of this heavenly sight!
Blow me about in winds! Roast me in sulphur!
Wash me in steep-down gulfs of liquid fire!
O Desdemòn! Dead Desdemòn! Dead! O! O!

Enter Lodovico, Cassio in a chair, Montano and Iago with officers

LODOVICO
Where is this rash and most unfortunate man?

OTHELLO
That's he that was Othello: here I am.

LODOVICO
Where is that viper? Bring the villain forth.

OTHELLO
I look down towards his feet; but that's a fable.
If you are a devil, I cannot kill you.

He wounds Iago

LODOVICO
Wrench his sword from him.

IAGO
I bleed, sir, but not killed.

OTHELLO
I am not sorry either; I'd have you live,
For in my mind it is happiness to die.

LODOVICO
O, you Othello, that were once so good,
Fallen in the plots of a damnèd slave,
What shall be said to you?

OTHELLO Why, anything:
An honourable murderer, if you will:
For naught did I in hate, but all in honour.

LODOVICO
This wretch has part confessed his villainy.
Did you and he consent in Cassio's death?

OTHELLO
Ay.

CASSIO
Dear General, I never gave you cause.

OTHELLO
I do believe it, and I ask your pardon.
Will you, I pray, demand that demi-devil
Why he has thus ensnared my soul and body?

IAGO
Demand me nothing; what you know, you know:
From this time forth I never will speak word.

LODOVICO
What! Not to pray?

GRATIANO
Torture will open your lips.

OTHELLO Well, you do best.

LODOVICO
Sir, you shall understand what has befallen,
Which, as I think, you know not. Here is a letter
Found in the pocket of the slain Roderigo,
And here another: the one of them imports
The death of Cassio, to be undertaken
By Roderigo.

OTHELLO O villain!

CASSIO Most heathenish and most gross!

LODOVICO
Now here's another discontented paper
Found in his pocket too; and this, it seems
Roderigo meant to have sent this damnèd villain,

But that, belike, Iago, in the nick,
Came in and satisfied him.

OTHELLO O the pernicious scoundrel!
How came you, Cassio, by that handkerchief
That was my wife's?

CASSIO I found it in my chamber;
And he himself confessed but even now
That there he dropped it for a special purpose
Which wrought to his desire.

OTHELLO O fool, fool, fool!

CASSIO
There is besides, in Roderigo's letter,
How he upbraids Iago, that he made him
Brave me upon the watch, whereon it came
That I was sacked; and even but now he spoke
After long seeming dead—Iago hurt him,
Iago set him on.

LODOVICO
You must forsake this room and go with us.
Your power and your command are taken off
And Cassio rules in Cyprus. For this slave,
If there is any cunning cruelty
That can torment him much, and hold him long,
It shall be his. You shall close prisoner rest,
Till the nature of your fault is known
To the Venetian state. Come, bring him away.

OTHELLO
Soft you; a word or two before you go.
I have done the state some service and they know it:
No more of that. I pray you in your letters
When you shall these unlucky deeds relate
Speak of me as I am: nothing extenuate,
Nor set down aught in malice. Then must you speak
Of one that loved not wisely, but too well;
Of one, not easily jealous but, being wrought,

Perplexed in the extreme; of one whose hand
Like the base Indian threw a pearl away
Richer than all his tribe; whose sùbdued eyes,
Albeit unusèd to the melting mood,
Drop tears as fast as the Arabian trees
Their medicinable gum. Set you down this:
And say, besides, that in Aleppo once
Where a malignant and a turbaned Turk
Beat a Venetian and traduced the state,
I took by the throat the circumcisèd dog
And smote him thus.

He stabs himself

LODOVICO
O bloody period!
GRATIANO All that's spoken is marred!
OTHELLO
I kissed you, ere I killed you: no way but this,
Killing myself, to die upon a kiss.

He falls on the bed and dies

CASSIO
This did I fear, but thought he had no weapon,
For he was great of heart.
LODOVICO O, Spartan dog,
More deadly than anguish, hunger, or the sea,
Look on the tragic loading of this bed:
This is your work. The object poisons sight:
Let it be hidden.

The curtains are drawn

Gratiano, keep the house
And seize upon the fortunes of the Moor,

For they succeed on you. To you, Lord Governor,
Remains the censure of this hellish villain:
The time, the place, the torture, O, enforce it!
Myself will straight aboard, and to the state
This heavy act with heavy heart relate. *Exeunt*